Shalom Ros

MW00443541

GOOD AND EVIL IN JEWISH THOUGHT

MOD Books   Tel-Aviv 61070

GOOD AND EVIL IN JEWISH THOUGHT
by
SHALOM ROSENBERG

English translation by John Glucker

No part of this publication may be reproduced, stored in a retrieval system, or transmitted in any form or by any means, electronic, mechanical, photocopying, recording or otherwise (brief quotations used in magazines or newspaper reviews excepted), without the prior permission of the publisher.

Copyright © 1989 by MOD Books
All rights reserved

English Series Editor: Shmuel Himelstein

ISBN 965-05-0448-6

Computerized phototypesetting & printing: Naidat Press Ltd.
Printed in Israel

MOD Books — P.O.B. 7103, Tel-Aviv 61070, ISRAEL

Rosenberg

Contents

PREFACE

In dealing with the present issue, the problem of good and evil in Jewish thought, we understand or feel, more than in all other cases, the limitations of the philosophical frame of reference and the occasional need for "the prudent" to "keep silent in that time." There are, it appears, some problems for which systematical philosophical analysis, with its clear and distinct ideas construed in the classic academic fashion, is insufficient. In such cases, people choose to express their feelings and their positions in other ways.

Rabbi Soloveichik has expressed his reaction to the problem of evil by way of action, and his answer to the question of evil is a *halachic* one. Others express their ideas and their reactions to the problem of evil by means of symbols; and this happens not only within the restricted area of philosophy, but also in the fields of artistic creation, literature and, of course, legend.

This issue has made many thinkers in the last few generations speak of the need for hermeneutics, not merely for philosophy. Hermeneutics means an attempt to form a discipline for the decipherment of symbols which takes myths, legends and folk-tales in full seriousness, since it is possible to discover in them approaches and positions which are no less important or significant than those which can be found in the great philosophical systems.

Thus, in dealing with the issue of good and evil, we have not restricted ourselves to academic philosophy, as exemplified in the

Middle Ages mainly in the writings of Maimonides, where things are written and set out in a systematic manner. We have also availed ourselves of legends of the Talmudic Sages, of the Kabbalah and Hasidism, and these are areas in the study of which the methods of academic philosophy are insufficient, and we have to look for other means of interpretation. This volume is indeed an experiment in the hermeneutic of positions and approaches, an effort to discover in them the reactions, thoughts and reflections of human beings faced with good and evil.

Shalom Rosenberg

I.

Good and Evil and Monotheism

In the following chapters, we shall deal with the problem of good and evil in classical Jewish thought. I should, perhaps, say a few words about the meaning of such terms as "Jewish thought" and "the classical age." I believe that Jewish thought constitutes something of a dialogue — a dialogue with the outside world and a dialogue of the Jew with himself. The Jew is, on the one hand, a person who accepts the authority of Sacred Scripture and of the sources of Judaism; but on the other hand he also accepts the authority of human reason and of his own rational faculties, and believes that he can arrive at a synthesis between these two sources of his views.

A discussion of Jewish thought is, in fact, a chapter in the study of general human thought. In this volume, we shall restrict ourselves here to one issue, the problem of good and evil, as reflected in classical Jewish thought. I am not sure that one can describe or define this area with precision; but in an attempt to do this, I have chosen a passage from a book which we shall meet with in a number of these chapters, *The Little Prince*. The book tells us of the galaxy from which the little prince arrived, and the author remarks that it is reasonable to assume that the galaxy from which the little prince came is the one known as B-612. It was discovered in 1909 by a Turkish astronomer, who came to an international congress of astronomers and gave proofs of his discovery. Nobody believed him, because of his exotic garments.

This is how adults behave. Fortunately for that galaxy, a strong ruler came to power in Turkey, and he commanded the citizens to change their exotic garbs for European dress. He even declared that anyone who transgressed against this law would be punished with death. In 1920, the same astronomer appeared once again and brought proofs of his discovery. This time, he came dressed in a very elegant European suit, and everyone accepted his view.

We shall deal here with classical Jewish thought, that is, with thought which is still dressed in exotic, non-European garments; but later we will find out that it is possible to change its garb. We will then realize that we have been dealing, in fact, with a chapter in the history of human culture, a chapter in man's struggle to comprehend the meaning of good and evil.

I shall not preface these chapters with biographical notices of the thinkers I shall deal with or with bibliographical references. My aim is to present the history of ideas as a struggle. Moreover, this work will not be like other works, especially in the field of natural science, which are not easily open to discussion and are above controversy. Here, the topics themselves depend on questioning and controversy. Even the investigation of the various opinions depends on controversy and argument.

When I began to study philosophy, I had a certain conception of what this discipline was about, but this conception later underwent a change. This change, which I wish to communicate to you, was clarified to me by means of a myth which I formulated for myself: Many centuries ago, there lived a man called Pythagoras. When people called him a wise man, he said: "I am not a *sophos* (a wise man); I am only a philosopher, a *philosophos*" (a lover of wisdom). Thus, beyond science, philosophy, which is a love of wisdom, came into being.

So far for the "historical" issue; now for the mythical ones. When someone enters one of the universities, he soon finds out that what people study there is, in fact, not philosophy, but "philosophography": a description of the various systems of philosophy. But as he proceeds with his studies, penetrates his area of research and integrates himself into it, he observes that there is not only philosophography, but also philosophographosophy; that is, that the exposition of the history of philosophy, the description of the various philosophical movements, or the analysis of philosophical views, all depend on certain philosophical positions; and even the objective study of other people's subjectivity is itself subjective.

In this volume, we will attempt, as far as this is feasible, to present the history of the idea of good and evil in Jewish thought. We will do this while ignoring the biographical and historical aspects of this idea. Maimonides deals with this idea in his *Guide to the Perplexed* when he discusses the classical example of this problem, in which he finds its most outstanding expression in the presentation of this problem in the Book of Job. In Book 3, Chapter 22 of the *Guide to the Perplexed*, Maimonides notes that there is a controversy among the commentators as to the Book of Job; some maintain that Job was a historical figure, while others claim that Job never existed, and that he is merely a parable. Maimonides sums up his brief historical remark with the words: "Finally, whether Job existed or not, an issue like his, which is always present, has perplexed all men who have looked into it." What really matters here is not the figure of the historical Job, but the problem with which the story of Job faces us. This is true not only for the presentation of this issue, but for its whole philosophical treatment. The various philosophers we shall deal with have expressed some fundamental positions. I shall attempt to present you with these positions in my survey, ignoring as far as possible the biographical and bibliographical aspects of this issue.

In the same context, Maimonides quotes a saying of the Talmudic Sage Reish Lakish: "The same one is Satan, the evil inclination, and the Angel of Death. They said: 'He descends and tempts, ascends and accuses, obtains permission and takes one's soul.'" What is described here is some kind of unholy trinity, a trinity of evil, identifying the three images in which evil makes its appearance to us: Satan, the evil instinct and the Angel of Death. In one of the following chapters, we will investigate the interpretation which Maimonides gave to this legend and its symbolism. At the moment, let us clarify one lesson which we can learn from this exquisite legend. What we learn from it is that the pair of concepts of "good" and "evil" has a number of different meanings. There is physical good and physical evil, represented by the Angel of Death — the evil of suffering, disease and extinction. Good and evil mean, in this context, pleasure and pain, life and death. On the other hand, we have here an allusion to another view and to an entirely different semantic signification of the words "good" and "evil," as represented by the evil inclination. This is no longer the good and evil involved in pain and pleasure, but good and evil in the context of transgression and commandment, of evil action and good action. Finally, a third possibility is hinted: evil depicted in the image of Satan. This significance is especially elaborated in the writings of philosophers — and I mean here the metaphysical significance of good and evil. We will discuss the meaning of this later.

Thus we have three distinct meanings of good and evil. We can add to them another one — the instrumental meaning. When, for example, a murderer asks a more experienced murderer whether the weapon in his hands is "good" for getting rid of so-and-so, he is using the instrumental sense of "good," forgetting all its other meanings.

But let us, for the moment, leave this "good" aside and concentrate on the first two meanings: good and evil as pleasure and pain, that is, physical good and evil, as against good and evil in the moral sense of fulfilling a commandment or transgressing it, of a good deed and a bad deed. This seems to us to be a clear and distinct division, although, as we will see, many philosophers, even if they were conscious of it, passed from one to the other of these two senses and confused the two.

By and large, we will deal here mainly with the meaning of evil in the first of these two senses, that of pleasure and pain; that is, with the manner in which man accepts the events of his life and the way in which he conceives of human history and of the life of this or that individual. At the same time, we will not — even if we wish to do so — ignore the other, moral significance of suffering.

12

One final remark. We will present the various views current in Jewish thought on this issue, and especially the views of Maimonides, who is a major figure in our debate, by confronting them with other views. We will find out that the history of these views has not followed a calm and steady course, but has always been accompanied by conflicts and contrasts. These conflicts can teach us a great deal about the nature of the idea with which we propose to deal.

The first chapter in the history of these conflicts will be elucidated with full attention to what is, without any doubt, the central core of Jewish Biblical faith as it has been conceived through the generations, including the Middle Ages. I refer, of course, to monotheism.

We all know that one of the central ideas of the Bible is monotheism: "Hear, O Israel, the Lord is our God, the Lord is one." But within the confines of this monotheism, and in the history of monotheism in general, I wish to draw the reader's attention to something which I would describe as three parts of the same play, or three acts in a continuing drama.

In the first act, which we will call the physical one, monotheism has to contend against views which maintain that each of the various sides of nature embodies, in essence, a different divinity. The Biblical God appears, in the context of this kind of monotheism, as Lord of heaven and earth. This is something of a protest, directed against the view which distinguishes between the god of heaven and the god of the earth.

It appears that, on the most primitive physical level, man refuses to believe that rain and droughts can come from the same source. Rain requires a principle of its own — a god of rain or storms — whereas drought must come from some different principle. The first act seems to us today to be rather remote, but one can hardly doubt that monotheism had to contend against it in the past. At the same time, this was only the first act.

In a later period, a second act is produced. The main problem now is not a physical one, but an ethical one. Thus, when monotheism is confronted by the Persian religion, the prophet

13

Isaiah says of God that He is the one who "forms the light and creates darkness, makes peace and creates evil" (Isaiah 45:7). Our Sages, when they formulated our Morning Prayers, changed "creates evil" into "creates all," to prevent us from reciting a blessing over the creation of evil. But there is no doubt that even when we say in our prayers that He "creates all," we imply that this "all" also includes, of course, evil. We will return later to this issue of evil and "all."

At the same time, we must realize that this verse and the form in which it is formulated mark a great and strenuous confrontation between the monotheistic Biblical faith and the dualistic Persian religion, which believed in the existence of two powers confronting each other, the power of good and the power of evil, or the power of light and the power of darkness. As against this view, the prophets felt bound to register their protest and claim that everything comes from one and the same source. As we will soon see, this protest gave rise to a new philosophical difficulty, for how could we understand evil as originating in God? But let us ignore this difficulty for the time being and emphasize only the ethical nature of this second act.

Thus we arrive at the third act, in which the confrontation takes place between monotheism and Greek philosophy. Greek philosophy was prepared to absorb monotheistic ideas, and it even produced some of its own accord; but it was unable to accept the view that matter and form could both originate in the same source. Thus a new, metaphysical, type of dualism was created. In this dualism, matter and form fill the function of two new gods, or two different origins; for it is inconceivable that what gave rise to form, or the origin of form, could also be the creator, or the origin, of matter.

Here we are faced with a totally new debate, which must have been inconceivable to our Biblical ancestors. This is the debate with metaphysical dualism, which is entirely different from the ethical dualism which characterized our last act.

This metaphysical dualism was revealed in its full force and with all its dangers in the Middle Ages, in the perplexities surrounding the familiar problem of creation out of something or out of nothing.

14

Jewish thinkers now asked themselves whether the Biblical description of creation out of nothing was to be taken as a literal truth, or should one, perhaps, understand this story in the sense of giving form to matter which had already been in existence — the process called by Medieval thinkers "creation of being out of being." Here we are clearly faced with a philosophical confrontation with the dualism of matter and form. As one of our late Medieval thinkers expressed this issue, to claim that there is, beside God, another independent element, matter, means that one believes in two divine powers. Thus, the same claim against which we had fought in the struggle against moral dualism now returned to face us in the new shape of metaphysical dualism.

In essence, then, monotheism had to engage in numerous struggles, while the nature of the struggle changed on each occasion. It would be hard to assume that within the confines of the first act — the struggle against pagan ways of thought — one could have raised the same sort of questions which we ask today in monotheistic thought. Pagan thought depicted a world with a multiplicity of images, a world which included demons and devils, powers of evil as well as powers of good, and this contrast existed, of course, even before the formation of Persian dualism. This world was depicted as a certain factual state of affairs. One who lives in such a world finds it difficult to ask questions or to complain to anybody, since this state of the world is regarded as a given fact.

It is when one reaches the stage of Biblical thought, when one is faced for the first time with the categorical statement that God is beyond nature, that He is the creator of nature and is responsible for everything which takes place — it is only then that one can raise Job's question and comprehend the courage required before one can come to God and ask Him about the cause of evil and the cause of suffering. When we read Job's words (Job 23:3-5), "Oh that I knew where I might find Him; that I might come even to His seat; I would offer my cause before Him, and fill my mouth with arguments. I would know the words which He would answer me, and understand what He would say unto me," we find in his words the cry of a man who is steeped in monotheistic thought, coming up to God with

15

arguments in the name of all those ideas which he had learned from the prophetic and wisdom literature, and according to which everything is God's creation. The question as to the nature of good and evil is thus to be understood, in terms of Jewish thought, in the light of this monotheistic idea.

Indeed, the great struggle which had to be conducted by monotheistic thought for many generations — one might almost say, a struggle which has been conducted until the present day — was the struggle against a position which embodies a synthesis between the contents of what I have called the second and the third acts — a synthesis between ethical dualism and metaphysical dualism. This is the position known to us as Gnosticism. The term "Gnosticism" is derived from the Greek word *gnosis*, which means "knowledge," and was a system of thought which was very widespread in the ancient world. This was a system or a view of the world which struggled against monotheism and competed with it in making converts. Even today we do not know enough about it. One can find in Gnosticism a certain synthesis between Persian belief, Platonic philosophy, and even Biblical views. The center of this system is the belief in two divinities. It is almost certain that the view we encounter here is that of the heretical Palestinian Sage Elisha Ben Avuyah, who believed in two deities. This brings us back to the famous dialogue between Rabbi Akiva and his pupils and Elisha ben Avuyah — a dialogue with a rival, which started at that period and continued in the Middle Ages and even into our age. I have little doubt that this system of thought also influenced the Nazi way of thinking and similar views. Gnostic thought divided the world into two realms, that of good and that of evil. But what was unique to it was its assumption that it was not only the physical world which was divided into these two realms, but even the supernatural, heavenly world was divided into two realms — the kingdom of God, and the kingdom of another divinity. We too are used to speaking of another power, Satan; but in the Gnostic thought he is much more than that: here, he is a god, the god who created this world, and who maintains a constant struggle with the other god, the good God.

Gnosticism could be described by the famous anti-Gnostic saying of our Sages, "No evil thing descends from above." This saying represents, without any doubt, the anti-Gnostic view *par excellence*, and is directed against those who maintained that there are, indeed, two divine powers in heaven. The nature of Gnosticism and its implications will occupy us in the next chapter.

II.

Two Divine Powers

We concluded our last chapter with an allusion to the system of thought which served as a challenge of the greatest importance to Jewish thought — the system, or doctrine, of Gnosticism. This system, as we already saw in the last chapter, took the form of an ethical and metaphysical dualism combined. In order to provide a more detailed interpretation of this system, we shall now go back to Plato and to Greek thought in general.

How does Greek philosophy depict the world? The world appears to it as composed of two levels. There is the changing and vibrating world, the world we live in, or the world of phenomena. Beside it and beyond it, the philosophers assumed, there is another world, a world which is static, which is all beauty, truth and goodness. This is the world of ideas.

If in the world of phenomena we encounter many things, in the other world there is unity. If here we see change, there there is rest. It is a world which we do not grasp through our senses, but only with our reason. This division, which was very fundamental and very well-known, was shared by many philosophers and accepted by Plato. Let us take an example. You are watching the television screen and observing a certain world. You know that many people live practically in that world, which is their only world, and are not aware that that world reflects another world, an external world, which is a real and true world; but watching the television screen sometimes and paradoxically prevents us from establishing a

18

contact with that world. In a similar fashion, Plato also believed that this world of ours, the world of phenomena, is in a certain sense also a screen, a mere projection of the real world. Just as there are many people now who try to persuade us to abandon the world of television and turn to the real world, so did Plato also attempt to persuade us that we should abandon our observation of the world of phenomena, the imaginary world, and turn upwards, toward the world of ideas, which is the real world itself, the world of the good, the beautiful and the true.

In Plato's terms, this world presents us with multiplicity and change, whereas in that world — and I shall refrain from using a term like "the other world," which has another significance in the world of ideas — there is unity. There we have the ideas in their pure form. In this world, there are many human beings, but they are made of matter, and therefore they are prone to illness, suffering and death. In the world of ideas, on the other hand, we have the idea of man, ideal man, which does not change and which is always equal to itself and identical with itself, inhabiting a world of eternity.

These are clearly two worlds. But we have not exhausted our description of them. We require something else — the search for God. Where, in this system, can we find God? It is interesting to remark that, in consequence of this assumption of two worlds, we could have reached the assumption that there are two divine natures. In fact, we could have assumed the existence of two gods — or, as we have just mentioned (and this expression appears very often in Talmudic literature, and probably hints at Elisha ben Avuyah's view), the existence of two divine realms of powers. For this world of ideas is depicted as a pyramid of ideas, culminating in the highest point, where we find the idea of ideas, or the idea of the good, the true and the beautiful. The many ideas are thus organized in a hierarchical fashion. There are ideas of numbers, ideas of mathematical functions and ideas of other types, and each is based on the other. From this point of view, it would be easy to arrive at God as the idea of ideas. But even if we assume the existence of God in this fashion, we can still ask ourselves *what is the origin* of this world of ours and whence it came to be. Here, a new figure makes its appearance, and I shall describe it with the Greek term which has by now become part of Western civilization, *Demiurge*. The Demiurge — *demiourgos* — is the creator or artisan, who looks at the world of ideas, and molds in matter shapes similar to the ideas, so as to make our world resemble the world of ideas as much as possible. Thus there is a figure which is all spirit and all intellect, the idea of ideas; but beside it, there is another figure, that of the Demiurge, which is very similar to our soul, which observes the world of ideas and molds in its shape forms in our world, as if it took the ideas and used them, like seals, to stamp their image on matter.

The potential for the formation of a dualistic view of the world is clearly revealed here. What we have here is, in the first place, the idea of ideas; but beside it we also have the Demiurge, that pristine creator. Judaism was faced, through these ideas, with a serious danger of an anti-monotheistic dualism. As I remarked in the last chapter, it appears that this was the view of Elisha ben Avuyah, who apparently believed in the existence of two such gods; one god who is all goodness and beauty but is alienated and remote from us, and another god, who is very close to us, but is entirely unlike the first.

This distinction is hard to explain in philosophical terms: it has to be experienced and made concrete. It might be helpful if I were to use an immediate association which has occurred to me — the characters in the television series, *Yes, Minister*. There we have two forces, as it were — on the one hand, the minister, and on the other hand, the director-general. The minister speaks for dreams or ideas, while the director-general is less alienated from reality — in fact he is the one who rules existent reality, guided by interests and instincts. Indeed, God as the idea of ideas on the one hand, and the Demiurge on the other hand, function, in this system of thought, in a very similar manner to the characters in this television program. It is as if we had a director-general who turns all the ideas of the minister into realities in the manner which seems to him to be appropriate. But his realization of the minister's ideas is in no way perfect. Let us take a very simple example. Let us say that a painter living now wishes to imitate a Rembrandt painting. If he puts before himself a Rembrandt painting and attempts to paint the same picture again, it is obvious that he cannot produce a perfect Rembrandt. But the truth is that even Rembrandt himself could not have painted a perfect Rembrandt, since the idea of the painting which Rembrandt had in his mind was no longer a perfect idea the moment he turned it into a reality. Here we meet with the fundamental ideas of classical Greek philosophy in general, and with its Gnostic direction in particular — the notion which maintains that the moment perfect ideas materialize and we attempt to impose them on matter, they are no longer perfect. It is as if a vision was taking shape, while reality was incapable of standing up to it.

How can we now assess the authority of the Demiurge? No doubt, in one way we can look upon his creations as good. On the other hand, one can have one's doubts. One can ask whether what we are faced with is not two gods, of which the one closer to us, the Demiurge, is evil.

Platonic thought met with monotheism in the thought of the Jewish philosopher Philo of Alexandria, who was the first to blend Platonic thought with monotheism and to create a synthesis between the teachings of Moses and a philosophical system. Philo, who by means of this synthesis created the whole phenomenon known as religious philosophy, attempted to solve this problem. He did it by means of a method which we shall not study here in detail, his doctrine of *logos*, of the word. By means of this doctrine he made the Demiurge totally dependent on God and subject to Him. He believed that this was in the spirit of Judaism: there may, perhaps, be angels, but they are of necessity subject to God's rule. The Gnostic, on the other hand, took an entirely different route. Gnosticism did not depict the artisan, the Demiurge, as subservient to God, but regarded these two figures as equal and contending divine powers.

The question now arises: we have depicted the two worlds of the Gnostic, but we have not even hinted at the place of man in this scheme. What, then, happens to man? One of the most fundamental elements of the whole of classical thought — both in Jewish thought and in this chapter of late ancient thought which we

21

are now discussing —is the conception, or feeling, that man is something of a small world; every man includes virtually everything which exists in the outside world. Man constitutes a *micro-cosmos*, a little world, in the sense that he is a small model of the whole of reality and of the whole of the cosmos. This idea originated, no doubt, in the elemental feeling of human complexity. Man is complex, but in this complexity of his he imitates the whole universe and constitutes a duplicate, as it were, of the whole world.

It follows, therefore, that if the world is cleft in two, these two parts also exist in man. In man, these two parts are his body and his soul. The body corresponds to the world of phenomena, the corporeal world, which changes and multiplies and has all the deficiencies we have mentioned, whereas man's mind (or, according to some, his soul) represents the higher world.

But it is precisely here that we meet with the most surprising element of the whole Gnostic system. For after all, what did the Demiurge do? He created a world, and he did it by imitating the higher world. But when he came to man, that artisan-god took a spark from that upper world and inserted it into him, and this is already much more than a mere imitation of that higher world. The implication is that man's soul belongs to another world and is only imprisoned here. Thus man's activity should be directed toward releasing himself from this prison. This is a pessimistic view, which regards the world as a jail, and assumes that man's duty is to attempt to set himself free from it. Such a view conceives of this world as being fundamentally evil. Pessimism assumes, in this system, a metaphysical basis, and is rooted in its concept of the divine. This world is fundamentally evil, and one has to escape from it.

In the previous chapter, I mentioned *The Little Prince*. It is interesting that toward the end of that book we have a conversation between the prince and the pilot, who has now succeeded in repairing his plane in order to return to his original place. The prince says to him: "I, too, am about to return today to my place of origin." Then he adds, sadly: "It is far more remote and far more difficult." The pilot is about to return to his place, but the little prince is also about to return to his own place, a certain bizarre and wonderful place which is hidden from us; a place to which it is far more difficult to return.

If I am allowed to indulge in an allegorical interpretation, I would say that we can read *The Little Prince* as yet another example of a wide range of literature which describes the destiny of the human soul. Let us observe the true meaning of what the little prince says. We overhear a conversation between a prince and a snake — one of those poisonous snakes which can kill a man within thirty seconds. "Is your poison efficient?" asks the little prince, "Are you sure that you will not cause me protracted suffering?" And, as the prince is about to depart, he says: "You will understand that the place is far too remote. I could not carry this body of mine with me. It is too heavy."

And indeed, the little prince is about to leave us now, as he is going to die. But he regards his death as a sort of return, as if he were about to return to his place of origin. The approach depicted here assumed a pre-existence of the soul. The soul's origin is in some other world, and it is to that world that it must return. What is surprising here is that it returns to that world by committing suicide.

Like many other parents, presumably, I offered *The Little Prince* to my children to read. But I am not sure now that I should not have paid more attention to this ending. Now I feel in it some tinge of Gnosticism. It is the feeling aroused in us by a man who comes up to us and says: "Know that I am leaving this world now and returning to my origin, and I am doing this by committing suicide." This is the world-picture of people and of thinkers who believe that they really do not belong to this world into which they have been hurled, against their will, and which is like a prison from which they wish to liberate themselves.

Once, when I was teaching the chapter of Maimonides which deals with our problem, one of my students asked me: "Why, then, does this philosopher not commit suicide?" The truth is that this question touches on one of the most sensitive points, which will enable us to comprehend the difference between various approaches to the nature of this world as embodied in the problem of good and evil.

In order to comprehend the full implications of this idea, let us compare it to an idea expressed by our Sages, in a midrash which one can find in *Avot of Rabbi Nathan* and in the *Midrash* on Psalms, referring to Ecclesiastes 4:13-14: "Better is a poor and wise child than an old and foolish king, who will no more be admonished. For out of prison he comes to reign; whereas also he that is born in his kingdom becomes poor." In the Hebrew original, the words translated as "out of prison" are *mi-beit ha-surim*, and would lend themselves to two interpretations: "out of the house of nettles and brambles" or "out of the house of prison." The latter interpretation — that which is also accepted by the English translation — is the basis of our rabbinic midrash: "The evil inclination within his bowels is king over man's two hundred and forty eight joints, while the good inclination is like someone who is incarcerated in a prison-house; for it is written 'for out of the prison-house he came to reign' — that refers to the good inclination".

Instead of the little prince, we hear in this midrash of a little boy who is poor and wise and not yet a king, facing a king who is old and foolish. The child, who is not yet a prince, is still in prison. At first glance, this seems to be once more the Gnostic image of the human soul, which is incarcerated in the body like a prison.

But there is one fundamental difference. The Rabbinic midrash which says that "'Out of the prison-house he came to reign' — that refers to the good inclination," implies, in fact, that it is this poor child who is to become a prince and a king. As our Sages say in other passages, the pious are those who make their good inclination reign over their evil inclination. The difference between the two views is interesting. According to the Gnostic view, the soul was stolen from the realm of spirit. It was taken from there against its will and put in prison here. According to the view of our Sages, which also maintains that the soul came from heaven, it was sent into the world because it has an aim and a function. It is at this point that we find a key to the question asked above: Why does the philosopher not take his own life? There are some views which regard the world as evil and conceive of suicide as liberation. These are the most extremely pessimistic views. Even in the pessimistic view of classical Buddhism, we cannot find this position. The Buddhists tell us, as it were: you, as a prisoner, have the option of escaping, but you should know that if you escape, you will be found out and taken back. Then, instead of being merely in a prison, you will be put in solitary confinement. Thus, even if you succeed in escaping, you will be hounded back, and your position will be even worse. It is simply not worth your while to try to escape by committing suicide. Even the underworld will be no refuge for you.

But the view of our Sages, which fought against the Gnostic world view, regarded suicide itself as an act of desertion and treason, as a misuse of your life, which is not your own, since you are merely an agent. It is quite likely that the soldier who is standing at the front line and fighting is not feeling happy, but he senses that he has been sent here not by some tyrant, but in order to fulfill a certain mission and to aim at the achievement of a certain end. Suicide will thus be desertion and treason, the turning of one's back to the target which faces him.

Be that as it may, the confrontation between the two world-views is a fact. The Gnostic view, when it appears in full force, claims that there are two divine beings in heaven, a good power and an evil power. In Persian thought, these two divinities were of equal weight and on the same level. Gnostic faith is different from the Persian view. To the Gnostic, these two powers are not equal. On the one hand, we have the good prince, and he is powerless and takes no interest in what is happening in the lower world. Beneath him is the Demiurge.

It was against such a view that Judaism had to fight. Throughout the generations, Jewish thought struggled against the Gnostic view, according to which Satan, or Evil, is an independent power. There are, of course, some places within Jewish thought where this seems to be the picture — especially in the literature of the Kabbalah. But I believe that one can say with a clear conscience that even in those places, we can detect at the base of these ideas and images the

25

fundamental view concerning the one single source of all reality and of all the worlds.

Sometimes it happens that we can detect traces of the Gnostic view in the realm of Jewish folklore. There is a story concerning a child-prodigy who was later to become a famous rabbi. One morning his father tried to wake him up in order to go to the synagogue, and said to him: "Go and learn from your evil inclination; for your evil inclination has already awakened, while you still want to sleep." The son, with the profound wisdom of children, answered: "Yes, but my evil inclination has no evil inclination of its own which would stop it from awakening." Thus, the boy was virtually, and unintentionally, expressing the idea that evil, or Satan, is no independent power and no independent ruler. It is no angel, not even a rebellious angel — although the idea of rebellious angels is found frequently in Jewish thought — but virtually a messenger. Thus, Rabbi Shneor Zalman of Liadi writes in his *Tanya*: "The Other Side itself has no doubts in matters of faith, but it has been given permission to confuse men with lies and deceits in order to increase their reward, as in the story of the Holy Zohar of the courtesan who tempted the king's son with lies and deceptions, with the king's own permission." Even "the Other Side," identical with Evil, is no more than a messenger of God.

Thus we are presented with two different possibilities of depicting the evil element, Satan. Gnosticism regarded Satan as the Demiurge, the evil and rebellious god, a cosmic soul whose activity is diametrically opposed to that of God, who is all goodness. But one can also regard him, as the large majority of Jewish thinkers have done, as someone who fulfills a task, not unlike a police informer who is "planted," who is, perhaps, a member of a subversive group or a gang of criminals, in whose nefarious activities he appears to participate, but in truth he is nothing but the messenger of the good force. Even when he fulfills an unpleasant command, he is still the messenger of the good force — for there is no other force above.

III.

Satan and Maimonides' Interpretation of the Book of Job

So far, we have been dealing with some chapters from the history of ideas in ancient times. We will now attempt to deal with the view of Maimonides. This will require some elucidation of Maimonides' terminology and philosophical method. The truth is that so far we have conceived this debate in its cosmic sense, as it were. But behind this cosmic problem there is undoubtedly a profound psychological problem, a human existential problem concerning good, evil and suffering. Maimonides, when dealing with this problem, approached it through a philosophical and ontological analysis, as we shall soon see.

In order to facilitate our approach to this subject, I shall cite an example from Chapter Seven of *Through the Looking-Glass*. The King says to Alice: "'Just look along the road, and tell me if you can see either of them.' 'I see nobody on the road,' said Alice. 'I only wish *I* had such good eyes,' the King remarked in a fretful tone. 'To be able to see Nobody! And at that distance too?'" This remark should demonstrate to us that even in a world like "nobody" or "nothing," we can see something positive, something which does exist — but that we should not make this mistake. This is a paradox which strikes home to the reader, thus making it easier for him to approach the ontological problem with which we shall soon deal.

What Maimonides tells us, in fact, is that the problem of evil in all its aspects is tied up with this problem of "nothing" — or, as he calls it, the problem of privation. When we examined the Gnostic system, we saw the existence in it of two powers, which I tend to illustrate in algebraic terms as the struggle between A and anti-A, or minus A (A and -A). What Maimonides wishes to tell us is that, in truth, good and evil are not like A and anti-A or minus A, but rather like A and zero A, or the total absence of A. This is the sense of evil as a privation. But Maimonides proceeds to warn us that we should not understand this privation as an absolute privation. We are not dealing with A as against zero, but with A as against zero A. It is as if we were to say that when we have been faced with something and now this something is absent, we understand it as a privation, and what we are facing is a privation *of that something.*

Maimonides connects this analysis with a philosophical debate he had conducted with the *Kalam*, a Moslem school of theologians, whom we shall only mention by name here. The debate between them centered on the question of how to understand this pair of concepts, good and evil — whether as something and nothing, or rather as A and minus-A, or in a similar fashion.

Let us assume that someone has entered a lighted room and turned the light off. Someone else now enters and asks, colloquially, "Who has made darkness by turning off the light?" Undoubtedly, what we have here is a mistake which could be labelled as a category mistake. It originates in the fact that we used language in a sub-standard, incorrect manner. Language is our greatest tool, but it is also a tool which assists us in deceiving others as well as ourselves. It thus happens that we also deceive ourselves in our relation to evil, since evil, in Maimonides' conception, is nothing; it is not "being," but a privation. It is in that which is absent that we must look for evil. Thus we return to that verse of Isaiah which we have already quoted: "I form the light, and create darkness; I make peace, and create evil." This verse, which, in our previous interpretation was used against dualism, obtains a different significance at the hands of Maimonides. Maimonides sees in it something like a manifesto concerning the nature of evil. Evil in comparison with good is like darkness in comparison with light. It is not the contrast between one being and another being, but between a being and its absence. It is something which is missing; and although you can say, apparently, that someone "made darkness," it is only language which is deceiving you, or by means of which you deceive yourself.

Thus we should realize that we do not really "make" darkness, since darkness is nothing but a privation. In the same manner, God, who is the source of all and of the whole of reality, is also the source of evil. The prophet says that God "forms the light and creates darkness, makes peace and creates evil," meaning, in fact, that God made light, and this is the creation of something positive. But in the nature of things, together with the formation of light, the possibility of darkness also arises. With the creation of good, there appears also the possibility of its privation, of evil.

Let us take an example. You are standing in the sun, but at the same time you are casting a shadow. The very fact that you are standing in the sun also makes it inevitable that there should also be a shadow. Why? because you are not transparent. The same applies to the fact that God created matter, which entails the appearance of evil, although creation itself is good. God created good, but evil necessarily also appeared.

Let me use a trivial, even banal, example, which will nevertheless help us understand, in concrete terms, the absurdity of dualistic ontology. For Maimonides, to speak of good and evil as two independent entities would have been as if we offered a child a partnership: come, let us bake a bagel: you supply the flour and water and I supply the hole. This example, banal as it may appear to be, would face us with the absurdity of comparing a void and an entity, evil and good. The hole is not something which exists in its own right. It is merely the result, and accompanying symptom, of a certain structure of the universe, which is itself good.

Thus, Maimonides' ontological analysis has a religious and theological aim on the one hand — to deny the existence of two divine entities — and on the other hand, to explain how the whole world originates in God, who is wholly good. Evil too has its divine origin, but not in its own essence, but merely as an accident. Evil is a necessary result of creation, and it has to exist. Its status, though, is like that of a shadow which appears together with the existence of a body. Just as the absence of things appears together with their existence, so also does evil make its appearance in the world.

Maimonides has formulated a general rule here, a principle which maintains that every evil is nothing but a privation. The cause of all evil and all suffering is nothing but privation and absence. This principle is divided by Maimonides into three levels of evil.

Suffering is no individual's privilege. But how should we even begin to discuss it and lay out a catalogue of kinds of suffering? Each person could come forward and propose his own private catalogue. It appears that Maimonides has an interesting division — one which could also be fruitful in some other areas — into three regions: the cosmic region, the social region and the personal region.

Some evils originate in the cosmic region — such as death, which is not even a human privilege, since other living beings also die. Diseases strike every living organism, and suffering is also a cosmic phenomenon.

The second region is the social one. The classic example of an evil in this region is war: war between societies, and war within a society. Although in some sense, war also exists in the animal kingdom and in other areas of reality, there is no doubt that it has some levels and dimensions which are particular to mankind.

There is also a third area: the evil which a man causes himself; man as his own worst enemy.

Maimonides' great thesis applies to all three regions, and maintains that in all three evil is nothing but a privation. Evil is the consequence of the basic fact that this world is something of a compromise. It is a compromise between creation, shaping and existence, which are good, and the fact that this existence takes place in matter, and matter involves, by necessity, imperfection.

If we remember the Gnostic view, which maintains that, for the Gnostic, the act of creation itself was evil and the Demiurge committed a sin when he created the material world, we will be able to comprehend the full significance of Maimonides' thesis, which maintains that the act of creation itself is good, and that the shaping itself is a good thing, but that, since this creation took place in this world, in matter which is imperfect, it has its imperfections.

In fact, Maimonides' doctrine faces us with an alternative: what would you prefer — a perfect spiritual world, but without you, or an imperfect world including yourself? Including yourself, with all the suffering which falls to your lot — but also with all the happiness which you may achieve. Including you, in the full knowledge that no man lives more than 120 years — but also in the full awareness that every single day and every single moment is a priceless treasure. What, then, would you choose? Maimonides believes that God made His choice on the basis of one single principle, the principle of good, since God is good in His nature, and He created the world out of His nature. You, the reader, have the opportunity to live your life, with all your limitations, and including the privation which follows from the nature of matter. It is probably for this reason that heaven is full of angels, billions of angels, who play their violins and harps and sing hymns to God; but at the same time, there are also human beings, who are less perfect than those angels, and they, too, are alive. They must live in the best manner possible for them, since this world — and this, perhaps, is a formula which will sum up Maimonides' thought on this issue — is, in the last count, the best of all possible worlds.

We all remember this formula from the writings of Leibniz, and also from Voltaire's great satire, *Candide*. But the idea itself may well have derived from a book which was well-known to Leibniz — Maimonides' *Guide to the Perplexed*. Maimonides' world-picture reveals a universe which is far from perfect — but it is the most perfect among the possible worlds.

Here we reach the third meaning of good and evil. We have spoken so far of physical good and moral good. Now we will deal with metaphysical good. Existence itself is good; to be is good in itself. We can imagine a world without human beings, or a world in which humans have not yet been created, and still say of it that it is good, that it is good in itself. In principle, one could almost say that God's first command when He created the world was not "Let there be light!" but "Let there be good!" which is nothing but "Let there be all that is possible!" Following on such an ontological command, a chain of being with an infinite number of links is created. Some of the higher links in this chain are, perhaps, perfect; but even we humans, albeit finite and imperfect, have a place in this link, and we also give expression to the good, as far as good is possible. Good is implied in the very fact that we are.

As against the pessimistic view of Gnosticism, we find here an optimistic philosophical view, which sees the world as good. Maimonides sums up his discussion of this issue with a Talmudic story he quotes in the name of Rabbi Meir. The Biblical story of the creation ends with the words "And God saw every thing that he had made, and, behold, it was very good" (Genesis 1:31). In Rabbi Meir's Bible, the last words, "and it was very good" (*ve-hineh tov me'od*) appeared in the version "and death was good" (*ve-hineh tov mavet*). According to Maimonides, this marginal gloss of Rabbi Meir was meant to teach us, by a slight change of Hebrew consonants, that even death is the result of the overall good of creation. For it is a fact that we find ourselves here in a world of matter, which is, in its very nature, dynamic — that is, it is based on plurality and on change. It is a fact that in such world we have to succeed each other. We have followed on our predecessors, and the day will come when others will succeed us.

Rabbi Meir's gloss is on a verse in the Biblical story of the creation. Indeed, death is involved in creation itself — and is prior to the story of the Garden of Eden. Hence, death is not the result of sin, but the consequence of the material nature of this world. Nature is "very good," and in this word, "very" we already have a hint to death, which is the inevitable concomitant of life.

So much for one side of the picture, which I would call cosmic. But it is important to note that Maimonides also introduces another idea, thus illuminating another side of reality. In order to understand this idea, I shall invite you on an excursion into Maimonides' interpretation of the meaning of the Book of Job. Maimonides was not only a philosopher, but also — even more so — a philosophical interpreter of Holy Scripture. One of the most exquisite examples of his Biblical exegesis is to be found in his conception of the Book of Job. We all remember the opening of the Book of Job, a scene which takes place in heaven. This scene has two parts. Satan appears twice before God, first, in 1:6, "Now there was a day when the sons of God came to present themselves before the Lord, and Satan came also among them." He came, so he tells us (1:7), "from going to and fro in the earth, and from walking up and down in it." In Chapter 2:1, Satan appears again: "Again there was a day when the sons of God came to present themselves before the Lord, and Satan came along them to present himself before the Lord." It seems that what we have here is two different scenes in the same drama, in which Satan comes twice before God. But Maimonides has a different view. In his exegesis, he maintains that what we have here is two different images of the Devil — if you wish, you can call them two different personifications of the Devil.

Maimonides was not only a philosopher, but an artist, with a sense of precision in his interpretation of Biblical writings. In the very beginning of the Book of Job, when we are told that "There was a man in the land of Uz" Maimonides detects a symbolism in these words — a symbolism which is reflected in the symbolic nature of the names. The name "Uz," is related to a Hebrew verb which means counsel or wisdom. Thus, we are already in the presence of wisdom, which is coming forward to raise the question of good and evil. Thus Maimonides teaches us to be precise in the interpretation of the hints facing us in the Biblical verses.

Of the Devil, when he appears before God in the first chapter, we are told: "and Satan came also among them," that is, among the sons of God. But the sons of God are the angels, and the angels are nothing but forces of nature — the sum total of forces at work in the world and of all things created in the world. They are "the sons of God," that is, entities which derive their origin, in a positive fashion, from God's creation. We are told that Satan came *among them* — as if he insinuates himself in their midst. He does not appear at this roll-call, for he has not been summoned. He is not one of the list of powers summoned by God, and by means of which He creates. But God cannot create a world without Satan also appearing *in it*. This is the same Satan who has come "from going to and fro in the land, and from walking up and down it." It is a Satan who has no power above, in heaven. His whole power and all his activities derive only from walking up and down the *land*. He is active only here below. Satan comes before God and speaks to Him, but his field of operations is here, on the land. Satan is the privation which is part of the material world.

Now, in consequence of the metaphysical interference between God and the Devil, Satan begins to torment Job. How does he do this? He makes fire and storm descend upon him and inflicts on him bandits and enemies. We are immediately reminded of what Maimonides has just taught us concerning the first two levels of evil: the cosmic level, which finds its expression in earthquakes and floods, fire and storm; and the social level, in which man hurts man: robbers and enemies come down on Job and attack him.

But there is also another Satan, and the words said to him are not exactly those said to Satan in Chapter One. In 2:1, we are told: "Again, there was a day when the sons of God came to present themselves before the Lord, and Satan also came among them to present himself before the Lord." This time, Satan appears as a force who comes to present himself before the Lord. He, too, has his positive origin in the act of creation. He, too, is a power created by God. Why? Since there is, apparently, another Satan, different from the first. So far, we have witnessed only one origin of evil — privation, shadow, zero. It is something which has no existence, and it is only we, by giving it a name, who gave it a semblance of being. But there is, it seems, another force. What is the nature of this force? It is a force within man, which is apparently a good force, but sometimes, when it cannot find its place in the hierarchy, can turn into an evil force. What is the nature of this force and of this Satan?

What we have here, indeed, is a depiction of a struggle which goes on within man. It is the struggle between reason and imagination — or, if you wish, you can call it man's rational and irrational faculties. When the irrational part of man has the upper hand, it can become dangerous. What happens in such a situation? Reason has ceased to reign in man, imagination has become too independent, and the irrational forces take over. This second Satan is, of course, related to the first Satan. Here, too, it is a privation, the absence of hierarchy and self-rule. This absence finds its expression in foolishness, and foolishness takes two different forms. This is one of Maimonides' most interesting ideas, and we can find it in the *Guide to the Perplexed* 3:11: "These are the evils which descend amongst men (that is, the evils which one man does to another), some on account of intentions and desires." One side of these evils draws its origin from desire. Another side originates in wrong and erroneous opinions and beliefs. But all of them, Maimonides maintains, are the consequence of privation — and he proceeds to give us an excellent paradigm which depicts all these evils:

> Just as the blind man, since he cannot see, and also since there is no one to show him the way, hurts himself and inflicts wounds on others, so are the sects among men: each of them, in the measure of its foolishness, inflicts great evils on itself and on others.

This is the tragic paradigm of the blind: human society is like a blind man who stumbles and hurts himself, but unfortunately, others are also hurt. This human evil, Maimonides points out, is the consequence of stupidity, of ignorance, of the domination of irrationality in man. Maimonides adds: "And if the wisdom were present there — wisdom whose relation to the human form is like that of the power of vision to the eye — all man's damages to himself and to others would have come to an end." Maimonides expects us, in the long run, to achieve the power of vision — the vision of our reason. This possibility is, in fact, man's final salvation; for, with the knowledge of truth, as Maimonides says in what follows, "Hatred and quarrels will disappear, and the damage man does to man will come to an end. And the prophet has already predicted this, saying: 'the wolf also shall dwell with the lamb.'" Salvation is thus nothing but the final victory of rationality over the irrational — and, when this salvation comes about, then "the earth shall be full of knowledge." This is the light we now lack, and this is the source which will help us overcome the evils and sufferings which have their origin within us.

Maimonides develops here an idea which was expressed, many centuries later, in a painting by the Spanish master Goya, which is entitled "The Sleep of Reason Creating Monsters."

IV.

Facing Pessimism

In this chapter we will continue to expound the view of Maimonides; but here we will present his view in its confrontation with those of other philosophical systems, against which he argues or struggles.

We have already mentioned the dualistic approach. There were however, other systems as well, and I wish to deal with three of them here in order to make Maimonides' position more intelligible. These three systems are that of Epicurus, or Epicurean philosophy; fatalism; and the most difficult of them all, pessimism.

Epicurean philosophy maintains that everything is accidental. The events which befall a man really are only an accumulation of accidents, and we should not search for a meaning in them. We have no right to interpret them.

As against this system, we have the fatalistic philosophy, which maintains that everything is destined and preordained. History, as well as the life of each individual, is nothing but the unfolding of events which were ordained before the creation, or before man's birth.

There are various approaches and different versions within the fatalistic approach. One can detect it, for example, in the hard pagan position, which maintains that the whole world is bound by a blind decree of fate, and even the gods cannot escape it. Another version, found in Stoic philosophy, is that the world is ruled by a strict determinism of a logical and physical nature, within the confines of which man can do nothing to change his fate. He has to accept the fact that he is in such a world in which all things have been preordained, and the only thing in his power is to learn to live with this knowledge. This is, in essence, the Stoic view. Both of these fatalistic approaches were current in the ancient world. The version of fatalism known to Maimonides was a third one, that of Islamic fatalism, especially in the variant known to us as "Ash'aryiah" — one of the schools of Islamic theology known as *Kalam*. Maimonides finds himself between two approaches, one of which maintains that everything is accidental, while the other maintains that everything is preordained. In the face of both of these views, Maimonides maintains that man is free and is, to a large measure, the architect of his own destiny. He is responsible for the good and evil — between which he makes his choice.

Let us cite an example of Maimonides' position in the face of the world of Islamic fatalism. The most forceful expression of his position is provided by Maimonides in his *Mishneh Torah*, in the fifth chapter of *Hilkhot Teshuvah*, where he asserts:

> Each man has the choice. If he wants to turn unto the road of good and be righteous, he has the choice to do so. If he wishes to turn into the way of evil and become wicked, he also has the choice to do so. Thus it is written in the Torah (Genesis 3:22) "Behold, man has become as one of us, to know good and evil."

These words of Maimonides have acquired the status of a classic formulation, asserting that man has "permission," or a free choice of the way he wishes to adopt for himself, thus making his own decision between the alternatives of good and evil with which he is faced. In the same fifth chapter, paragraph 2, Maimonides adds:

> You should not conceive in your mind that thing said by the foolish among the gentiles and many of the boorish among the people of Israel, that God decrees, from the moment a man is born, whether he should be righteous or wicked.

Man, indeed, is the architect of his own fate. But there are some who oppose this view, and Maimonides uses the strongest language against them, calling them fools and boorish. At the same time, though, he draws a very interesting distinction, which is worth considering.

Maimonides speaks of "the foolish among the gentiles," and "the boorish (*golmim*) of the people of Israel." This is no accidental distinction, but something which he wishes to express. Maimonides was aware that there were some religions — especially those varieties of Islam which we have just mentioned — which assumed that man is not free, but that it is the will of God which preordains everything. These religions were faced with an interesting dilemma of monotheistic thought. Man's freedom of action was presented by them in contrast to God's sublimity and omnipotence — and in this ideological struggle, God's omnipotence wins the day: God's omnipotence at the expense of human freedom.

This position is designated by Maimonides by the brutal name of "foolishness": these are "the foolish among the gentiles." But Maimonides also knows that there are some among the people of Israel whose approach is similar, and he calls them "most of the boorish (*golmim*) of the people of Israel." This is a subtle distinction. Maimonides takes the word *golem* (translated by us as "boorish") from the religious laws concerning the defilement of vessels, which also deal with vessels which have not yet been finished. In the eyes of Maimonides, those Jews who believe in determinism and fatalism are also "unfinished Jews," who have not yet attained a full comprehension of Judaism, since theirs is an approach which is alien to that of Judaism. If, indeed, there are Jews who believe that destiny is fixed and they have no power of changing it, they are "unfinished vessels." *Golem* in Hebrew also signifies a chrysalis, a stage in the development of the butterfly. Thus, these people have reached an intermediate stage in their religious development, but they have not reached the final stage. They are not yet free as a butterfly, but are bound up like a chrysalis. This bound-up stage of a *golem* is a stage which we must overcome. The balance here is tipped unambiguously on the side of free choice and of the view which emphasizes man's responsibility for his actions as the cause of his own good and evil.

In the third paragraph of the same chapter, Maimonides demonstrates this view. After the giving of the Law, we read in Deuteronomy 6:29 (a verse later quoted by Maimonides himself):

"O that there were such a heart in them." What is interesting is that these words are spoken by God Himself. It is as though God Himself were saying: "May the heart of the Children of Israel remain as it is now." Maimonides learns from this that, even in the eyes of God, the future is open. In that "prayer," God is depicted as if He is awaiting man's own decision as to the manner in which he will choose between good and evil.

So far, we have observed Maimonides polemicizing against the option of fatalism, one of the two options which confronted him. On the other side, Maimonides also fights against the Epicurean position, which regards history, nature and the life of the individual as something purely accidental. His words against this Epicurean position can be found in *Mishneh Torah*, Chapter 1 of *Hilkhot Ta'aniyot*, third paragraph. Reminding us of the need to pray, to cry to God and to fast in times of tribulation, he writes:

> If they do not cry and blow the horn, but merely say that this thing which has befallen us is part of the way of the world, and this trouble has come by accident, this is a cruel practice, which will make them hold on to their evil deeds and make this trouble breed more tribulation. For thus it is written (Lev. 26:27-8), "And if you ... walk contrary unto me; then I will walk contrary unto you also."

These words are said in the reproach (the *tokhehah*) to the children of Israel, and the Hebrew word translated as "contrary" (*keri*), can be interpreted as "accident." This is how Maimonides explains these verses, taking them to apply to the view that history evolves in an accidental fashion. He explains our verses to mean: "If you behave as if every event which takes place is an accident which is none of your making, I will treat you in the same manner, and the command of your destiny will be taken out of your hands." Maimonides concludes that man should not think that everything is a matter of accident and that he has no power of acting or of changing things. In the face of fatalism, as well as in the face of the claim that everything is accidental and one can change nothing, Maimonides offers us a position which can be called activism.

But this activism is limited, of course, to man's capacities. Here

40

we come to the third theory against which Maimonides struggles, the theory of pessimism. It is not very difficult to find examples of pessimistic thinkers. As we will see later, the classical example is Buddhist philosophy. The most outstanding modern example is the philosophy of Arthur Schopenhauer. The example before Maimonides was an outstanding Moslem — or, in fact, heretical — thinker of the tenth century, Abu-Bakr al-Razi, who believed that the world was the result of a mishap, or of the sins of a certain cosmic soul which desired to be bound with matter. We have already noted a similar process described by the Gnostic dualists, but Abu-Bakr assumed, even more forcefully, that existence itself was an evil.

It might be interesting, in this connection, to skip a few centuries and look at the view of one of the religious thinkers of the last generation, Rabbi Abraham Isaac Kook. We will soon find that Rabbi Kook continues the thread of thought begun by Maimonides. In presenting us with the pessimistic option, he speaks of four possibilities which exist in the mind of man, or four possible positions concerning evil. The first of them is the absolute desire for evil, represented by the pagan approach. For a reader of our own generation, I assume that the classic example of this approach is to be found, not in ancient times, but in the neo-pagan ideology of the Nazis. This is the position which proclaims a complete reversal of values and believes that one should not only make use of evil, but also identify with it.

Compared with this first approach, which makes its pact with evil and preaches a reversal of values, the second approach recognizes evil in all its wickedness. This is the position which accepts the fact of evil being evil, maintaining that one cannot live with it. Disappointment with the world drives it into absolute despair, and its desire for salvation is turned into a wish for annihilation. This, as Rabbi Kook understands it, is the position of Buddhism.

But there is also a third view, which is designated by Rabbi Kook as half-despair. This is the view which maintains that one should hand over, in desperation, matter and the social world into the hands of evil, in order to salvage the inner life, which is the good and noble aspect of life. In the view of Rabbi Kook, this is the position of Christianity, which has agreed, in its half-despair, to accept the idea that this world is an evil world, and that the only thing which can be saved is man's spirit or soul.

Thus we are faced with different positions, of complete or partial despair. What is common to all of them is the claim that this world is evil, that it embodies the power of evil, and that it is a place where we cannot overcome evil. We are immediately reminded of al-Razi's version as presented by Maimonides, which claimed simply that, in a purely empirical fashion, one can find out that there is far more evil than good in the world, and therefore that the world itself is evil.

Maimonides maintained that this pessimistic approach made three mistakes. The first one, in Maimonides's terminology, is "man's mistake in himself;" i.e. man's imagining that the whole world exists for his sake alone. The pessimistic approach thus errs in being anthropocentric; in assuming that man is the center of all being, and that the whole of reality was not created except for the purpose of serving him. Thus, if man is affected by evil, the whole of reality becomes evil in his eyes.

The second error is the misunderstanding of "the nature of this matter." It is bound up with the claim that there are various possibilities of existence, and that other worlds, better than our world, are possible. This, in Maimonides' opinion, is a purely unrealistic and imaginary approach to the world.

The third error is ignorance of "the First Designer, who created everything which can be, and being itself is undoubtedly good." When we fall into this error, we do not understand that being itself is good, and that it has to be judged beyond the existence of man. What Maimonides is telling us is that when we judge the whole of reality from the point of view of our existence as human beings, we are likely to arrive at a pessimistic conclusion. But this is a mistake, since we have to come out of the narrow confines of our life and judge the whole world and the whole of reality from a cosmic point of view.

Maimonides draws our attention to the fact that, in the first chapter of the Torah, Genesis 1, we are told of the creation of many things. Each day, we are told, something different was created; and of each of these acts of creation, even before the creation of man, we are told that "God saw that it was good." This means that there is good, for example, in the existence of light — even before the creation of man. There is good in the existence of flowers, of trees, of grass, of whales and of animals — even before the creation of man. No doubt, when man was created, it was said of him as well that "it was good." Moreover, when man was created and the whole of creation could be seen in its entirety, God said "that it was very good." This was, as it were, an estimate of the world in its entirety. But one should not forget that there are good things even outside man. The cardinal sin of the pessimist consists, in Maimonides' view, in his assumption that everything should be judged from man's egotistical point of view. Of course, if man believes that he is the guest of honor at the banquet and everything has been made only in his honor, he can complain about the quality of the banquet. But if we accept that there are also other creatures, living beings, plants, stars — and one can add stones and angels — which are above and below man, and each of which has its own place in that great chain of creation — then we will have to say, as the Torah does "and God saw that it was good." We will have to admit that reality itself is good. This is also the true meaning of the verse (Prov. 16:4) "The Lord has made all things for Himself." In Hebrew, one can interpret the last expression as "for *him*self" — for the sake of God Himself — but also as "for *it*self" — each thing for its own sake, as though each thing were an end in itself, and was not made to serve man. Hence we must understand that evil is the consequence of an optical illusion, of an egocentric perspective. It is usually maintained that the standpoint of religion is anthropocentric, that it turns man into the crown of creation and the paragon of creation. This is true of some systems of religious thought — perhaps of the system of Rav Sa'adiah Gaon or of some systems of the Kabbalah — but it is not true of Maimonides' system. Maimonides emphasizes again and again, often in the most explicit manner, that this conception is an error which we must overcome and discard.

In this context, Maimonides produces a parable which has obtained the status of a classic example, and is repeated in Yadayah Ha-Penini's *Bekhinot Olam*. "And this," says Maimonides, "is like the case of an artisan, who made tools which weigh as much as a huge lump of iron, all in order to produce one needle which weighs no more than one grain." We, of course, would find it hard to imagine that a craftsman would take a ton of iron in order to make of it one small needle. This would be a wasteful act. The same applies to the cosmos. Man is no more than a needle, a small grain in a whole universe. He is surrounded by a stupendous world, and judging that cosmos to be evil from the point of view of man is a distortion which we should overcome.

Such is Maimonides' rationalist view. No doubt — and we will see in what follows — it was far from satisfactory to all subsequent thinkers, since its consolation is only partial. It does, indeed, solve the problem of evil, but it does not answer man's existential problem. It solves the problem of evil at the price of a reduction in man's stature in the universe. There is little doubt that this conception of Maimonides, which accords with his overall philosophical view, has some points of contact with the view of modern science concerning the open universe, the infinite distances within it, and the feeling of man that he is a mere reed on the shores of a vast ocean.

Had Maimonides stopped at this point, we could have judged him to be merely an orthodox Aristotelian, merely following in the steps of his Greek master. But in his comment on the Book of Job Maimonides adds an interesting detail: he maintains that Job represents Aristotle. But the true answer is to be given, not by Job, but by Elihu, Job's friend. The position of Job = Aristotle did not satisfy Maimonides. In order to comprehend this position of Maimonides, let us return to another chapter of *The Little Prince*. The prince has met with a king who claims that he is omnipotent, and that he can create facts which would change reality. Faced by this self-presentation, the prince asks the king "And do the stars obey you?" "Of course", said the king, "they obey me and fulfill my commands immediately. I cannot stand lack of discipline." The prince then asks the king, if he is willing to oblige, to command the sun to set — for the sunset was always one of his favorite views. The king answers: "If I were to command one of my noblemen to fly from one flower to another like a butterfly, to compose a tragedy, or to turn into a sea-bird, and that nobleman refused to comply with my command, who of us two would be the guilty party, the nobleman or myself?" "You," said the little prince.

Exactly. One can require of each man only what he is capable of doing. Government can only be based on the foundations of reason. The king complies with the little prince's request, and orders the sun to set. But he does this only after he has looked into a hefty volume of the order of times and says: "This will happen approximately this evening, about seven forty. Then you will see with your own eyes how my commands are obeyed and fulfilled." Thus it transpires, at the end of the day, that reality is, in fact, fixed, and the king — that is, God —cannot change it.

This was also the position of the more extreme Aristotelians. But Maimonides, unlike Aristotle and unlike Job, believed that despite all, there was some opening for change. This change originated in Divine Providence, which finds an expression in human reason. This was also the position of Job's companion Elihu. The ideas of providence and of salvation distinguished Maimonides from Aristotle. We will deal with this issue later.

V.

The Best of all Possible Worlds

The last chapter dealt with the challenge posed to us by pessimism. Pessimism maintains that existence is an evil, and — what is even worse — that the will to exist, that personal instinct which is so familiar to each of us, is the very source of evil. We have looked into a number of versions of pessimism. We mentioned the thousands-of-years-old version of Buddhism, which sees in the cycle of existence an evil, regards the escape from life as its aim, and preaches liberation from the regularity which reigns in the world. It is a version of pessimism which dreams of an end to the will, of its death or disappearance in nothing, in the Nirvana.

Some modern views were formulated which were greatly influenced and fascinated by Buddhism, such as the philosophy of Schopenhauer, or of his pupil and disciple, Eduard von Hartmann. These regarded the will as "the thing in itself" in Kantian terms, and believed that this thing in itself, reality as it is — which is nothing but the will — should be annihilated by us. Von Hartmann visualized a picture of a dualistic battle, which is similar, in an interesting manner, to an idea which also appears in the writings of Nathan of Gaza, the "prophet" of the false messiah Shabbetai Zevi. According to von Hartmann, in this world there is a struggle between the will, which is evil, and wisdom, which is good. It is the will which desires our existence, whereas wisdom, which is good, wants to bring us back to evanescence, to non-existence, to what could be described as the terrible "annihilation," turning us into

46

nothing. In fact, wisdom wishes to repair the evil in this universe by means of turning the world from being to non-being. This shall be the end of us all, and at the same time also the last triumph of good over evil.

In the face of such pessimistic positions, we present the view of Maimonides, a philosophical view which can be described as fundamentally optimistic. This is a position which sees in being and existence themselves a good, and, regarding the great chain of being, maintains that the world was created by means of one command of God, "Let there be good" or "Let there be all." This is the crucial command, since these two are identical. It is a position which realizes that man is not the crown of creation or its purpose, but that the purpose of creation is in everything. Each single thing is an aim in itself — or rather, the whole of reality is an aim in itself — and man is only one link in the great chain of being.

At the same time, this is a sober optimism, a limited one. For it adds a third premise, the claim that this is the best of all possible worlds. The first part of this premise is the assertion that being and existence are in themselves good, although men often do not understand this. This embodies the claim that the very existence of the world is an act of Divine favor toward us. This idea found a wider expression in the writings of Jewish philosophers of the fourteenth and fifteenth centuries, and became a fundamental tenet of their systems. Thus, one of the last great Jewish philosophers in Spain, Rabbi Hasdai Crescas, maintained that the world was created as an act of mercy and love. The Biblical words "and it was very good" are thus an expression of a judgment of the whole universe — not on God's creation, but on that act of mercy and love which finds its expression in the world.

Another thinker, Rabbi Isaac Aramah, author of the famous philosophical commentary on the Bible, *Akedat Yitzhak*, depicts for us a world which is not only good, but also beautiful; a world which was created not only to arouse our ethical sentiments, but also our aesthetic feelings. "For the Holy One, blessed be He," writes Rabbi Isaac Aramah,

could have created man without the sky and the stars, without all those plants and animals. But this would not have been such a fine and exquisite existence as it is the way it was created, and He, blessed be He, chose to make it the most perfect and exquisite existence.

According to Rabbi Isaac Aramah, therefore, the world is not only good but also beautiful, and it was created to include things which are apparently superfluous. Colors and hues do not, perhaps, have any productive function, but they have an aesthetic aim in themselves. In the view of Aramah, the world is an orchestra. He writes: "According to the simile and the parable we have used, He wished to perfect the harmony of the music of the world in its creation." It is as if the whole world is playing a melody, and each part of the world is an instrument in the orchestra playing this melody. If one single instrument were to be missing, the whole world, the whole of this orchestra, would be lacking.

All these are expressions of a feeling of optimism concerning the goodness and beauty of the world. But we should emphasize again that this is a limited optimism, and the limitations are inherent in the fact that the world was created in matter. This means that — given the limitation implicit in the fact that the world was created out of matter — it is the best of all possible worlds. It is possible, of course, that other worlds might have existed — but these would have been purely imaginary worlds which find no expression in matter.

The Medieval Jewish philosophers, from Maimonides onwards, explained in this spirit a well-known legend in *Midrash Bereshit* (*Genesis Rabbah*): "'And there was evening and there was morning': Rabbi Abbahu said: 'Hence we learn that the Holy One, blessed be He, was building worlds and destroying them, until He created this one.'" The verse, "and there was evening and there was morning," hints to us that there were apparently worlds before the present one, but these worlds were destroyed by God because they were not to His liking. "And He said: 'These ones appear to Me right, and those do not appear to Me to be right.'"

One can understand this aggadah at its face value — indeed, some modern thinkers see in it a hint to some modern ideas concerning the geological process, as this emerges from scientific research. This is far from the interpretation of our Medieval philosophers, and especially from that of Maimonides. Maimonides and his disciples saw in this legend not a report of something taking place in the external world, the world before us, but of something which happened, as it were, in God's own thought. There were, as it were, different projects. The words "building worlds and destroying them" refer to the various possibilities encountered by the Cosmic Architect, God. There were numerous possible worlds, but God "destroyed" them, all but one, and was left with this world. All those worlds which were destroyed — all those plans, to use our own language, which were rejected — are alternative worlds, but they are worse alternatives than the existing one. Thus we are faced with one true choice. The same Rabbi Isaac Aramah, author of *Akedat Yitzhak*, spells this out: "For His knowledge of all sides is ... construction, and His decision in favor of the side which appears to Him to be the best is the destruction of the other sides." In his Medieval idiom, Rabbi Isaac Aramah is telling us in the most explicit manner that we have a very large number of possibilities, numerous worlds which were destroyed — that is, rejected — and that we are left with our own world, a world which this kind of optimist regards not as wholly good, but as the best among the possible worlds.

Had we remained at this point, we would, in fact, have identified with the position of the king who answers the little prince's request by saying: "I cannot make a new sunset for you now; I have to look at my astronomical tables first, and in accordance with them, I shall command that star, the sun, to set" — which is exactly what he proceeds to do.

So far, it appears, we have been faced with the Aristotelian view of the limitations of Divine power. At the same time, we should not ascribe this view to Maimonides, for, to the description of Maimonides' approach which we have so far provided, we should now add another detail, and this will bring us to an area with which we have not been concerned so far.

We have seen that the discussion of good and evil brings us, in practice, to other areas — to a discussion of purpose, the purpose of

49

the world; to a discussion of ethical problems and the problem of divine providence, with which we opened this book; and to questions which can be called, in the classic Jewish terminology, questions of trust in God: how am I to live, and what can I expect of life? The issue with which we shall now deal is called, in the terminology of philosophy, "theodicy." This is very close to the Jewish *halachic* term of *Tziduk Ha-Din*, "justification of God's decree," but what we are discussing here is not justification of God's *decree*, but a justification *of God*, and this is the dirrerence between the philosophical and the *halachic* terminology.

Essentially, what we are trying to examine is the place of evil and good from the cosmic, or theological, point of view, and ask how these can have their origin in God. This brings us, in fact, close to another problem which is tied up with that of good and evil — the problem of salvation. In a way, we could have placed these two issues at opposite poles of each other — on the one hand, good and evil, and on the other, the diametrically opposed end, salvation. For what, after all, is the meaning of good and evil? We find ourselves, perhaps, in a situation similar to that of Adam and Eve, eating of a tree of good and evil. We will not enter here into problems of biblical exegesis —although we will return later to the story of the Garden of Eden. Let us take this story, for the moment, in one of its possible senses. We eat fruits in which good and evil are mixed. We have pleasure and pain. The average reader would not, undoubtedly, be an extreme pessimist like Schopenhauer, nor would he be the extreme optimist ridiculed by Voltaire in *Candide*. He would know that each of us bears his own burden. He would also realize that one need not, or one does not wish, to exchange his own burden with that of someone else. There is, in our lives, a mixture of good and evil.

But as against this mixture of good and evil, we also have another conception which we know from a number of sources, but especially from the Grace after Meals: "a day which is all good." We speak of a world which is all good, of a vision which represents a triumph over evil and the disappearance of evil. This is, in a nutshell, the concept of salvation or redemption.

We may thus proceed to say that our understanding of good and evil in the world is bound up with two concepts: a) that of divine providence, the profound meaning of which is: power over evil in everyday life; b) even more so, with the idea of salvation, of victory over evil at the end of days. When we speak of the best of all possible worlds, we must remember that even the best of all possible worlds is not a perfect world, and we can continue this thread of thought and dream of the perfection of the world, of a certain kind of reality in which, to use the words of the prophet (Isaiah 25:8) with a slight alteration, "He will swallow up evil in victory," a reality in which evil will no longer exist.

Without entering too deeply into this issue, let us only say that if we were to attempt to draw up a catalogue of the various ideas of salvation, we would have to begin — as I once suggested in one of my articles — by drawing up a catalogue of tribulations. There is hardly any doubt that anyone who wishes to study the idea of salvation will soon discover that he is dealing, not with a single problem, not with the material of a seminar, but with a whole library or a life's work. The idea of salvation is so complex and so variegated, that one has to restrict oneself to a certain vantage-point in order to deal with it. In one of the earlier chapters, I suggested that we could deal with the problem of evil according to three areas in which evil has its power —the cosmic region, the region of history, and the region of individual life. It is in these three regions that I will also try to deal with the idea of redemption.

In the region of history, we discover both national and international evil, the suffering of the people of Israel as well as the sufferings of the whole of mankind. Beside it is the cosmic region, where evil predominates by means of disease and death in the whole living world. Then there is the region of the individual, the sufferings of each individual human being. It is interesting to see that Maimonides does not accept the possibility of cosmic redemption; that he does not believe, or expect, that there should be any changes in the order of nature as God created it. He does not conceive of a situation in which human beings will no longer die. He does, however, dream, with the certainty of faith, of a day in which

51

man will reach the fullness of his historical development. This is the core of Maimonides' idea of the end of days.

There is, of course, also the individual eschatological idea of the survival of the individual soul and the life to come. But beside this individual vision, Maimonides also had a historical vision: human history as a whole must reach its fulfillment. To some extent, one could say that Maimonides saw in salvation the end of the process of creation. In fact, at the very moment when the ideal society has come into being, the process of creation will reach its end. We are merely a product in the first stages of its manufacture. In human society today — as we noted earlier — we still have the reign of the irrational, of crime, corruption and of human stupidity. The day will come when we reach the final stage of our development and form a just and perfect society, in which there will no longer be lack — not in the simple sense of this word alone, but also in its most sublime sense. There will be no lack of bread, but also no lack of wisdom. It is then that man will reach the fulfillment of all his possibilities. He will be able to realize himself to the fullest and to arrive at the ideal of humanity. This is Maimonides' conception of historical salvation.

This, then, was the approach of classical Jewish philosophy. And here I wish to attempt once more to lead the reader, by jumping over a few centuries, to Rabbi Abraham Isaac Kook. Let us consider the reaction of Rabbi Kook — whose starting point is that of the Kabbalah and Hasidism, although he was open to any modern point of view — to this classical philosophical position.

We have already seen how Maimonides depicts for us evil and Satan as a zero, a privation, a problem which our material existence poses for us. This appears to us to be the optimistic point of view which we contrasted with the pessimistic one.

Rabbi Kook refers to the same position, but what he says may appear to be somewhat strange, although it embodies a very profound truth. Rabbi Kook writes in *Orot Ha-Kodesh*, Part 2: "The existence of evil in the universe, whether it be general or individual evil, whether it be ethical or practical, in whichever description it may be found —as soon as we survey it in general and in detail, we find in evil order, an organic whole, and structure, so that it cannot be referred to as accidental."

I ask the reader to make an effort to understand the words of Rabbi Kook by penetrating behind the style of the beginning of this century, which has been transformed since. In a paradoxical manner, Rabbi Kook says, when we consider evil — whether general evil or individual evil, whether moral evil, the evil which a man does, or practical evil, the evil which a man suffers — we observe order, an organic whole, and structure. What Rabbi Kook wishes to emphasize is that "the Other Side," or evil, is no mere accident. It appears before us as something real, as something which virtually has the same structure as the good. We have noted how the optimistic philosophical view discovered in the world some structure which is good, but beside it there was accident, and in some accidental manner, evil also makes its appearance. But this is not the picture we have here. Here, says Rabbi Kook, we must understand that we are faced with evil with its full structure and in its full force.

Apparently, this is a bad state of affairs. But here we learn something of the paradoxical side of Rabbi Kook's doctrines. The truth is, as Rabbi Kook proceeds to explain to us, that evil in the sense of Maimonides is an evil of which we will never be able to rid ourselves. It is a privation which will not vanish even at the end of days. Rabbi Kook, like many philosophical and Kabbalistic thinkers who were not satisfied with Maimonides' limited optimism, dreamed of a world which will truly be all good, a world in which we will overcome even the cosmic evil which is embedded, as it were, in our world, a world in which "the wolf also will dwell with the lamb" will be no mere allegory concerning the political relations between the Soviet Union and Poland or Hungary, but in which nature will truly be transformed.

What Rabbi Kook tells us is that as long as we conceive of evil only as a privation, as an accident, we turn it into something with which we will always have to live. For Rabbi Kook himself, on the other hand, evil is a reality — but it is a reality which is capable of disappearing, and which will be abolished when the world is

53

perfected. Rabbi Kook's principal thesis — which sums up much of the thought of the Kabbalah and Hasidism, with which we will deal later in more detail — maintains that there are two things in the world: there is perfection, which is God, and there is also perfectability, something which aims at becoming perfect and desires to become perfect. In a paradoxical manner, let us now return to the legend of Rabbi Abbahu which we quoted above. For Maimonides, it is clear from the legend that God has chosen the best of all possible worlds. For the sort of thought which we have been trying to examine here, though, God has not chosen the best of all possible worlds. He chose, intentionally, a world which is not perfectly good, which has not yet reached its perfection, so as to allow human beings to turn it into a more perfect world. Thus, the cosmos contains a certain mark of imperfection, without which reality is not perfect. It is a world of "becoming perfect." It has in it, as it were, the possibility of becoming perfect, and it is our task to perfect it, since we alone are capable of making it better.

Thus, the improvement of this world is made into a task incumbent on man, a task still incumbent upon us. This world is admittedly not the best of all possible worlds, but it is a good world, since there is a final stage, a final point, which we can approach and to which we can come closer and closer, and at that point death will vanish forever.

VI.

The Tree of Knowledge of Good and Evil

When we discussed Maimonides' exegesis of the book of Job, we saw that, according to Maimonides, there are two images of Satan. The first Satan, who we described as uninvited, represents the problems implied by the very existence of matter, the evil born out of our material being. This first Satan is privation.

But in the second chapter of Job, a second Satan appears. This is already a different Satan, and with him, we come closer to another figure to which Maimonides refers, and who is already familiar to us from Talmudic and Midrashic literature — the figure of Sammael. In observing this figure, we touch on what is perhaps one of Maimonides' most exquisite and interesting theories, a theory which was to exercise a crucial influence later on the development of Jewish thought. This is a theory which illuminates the other side of evil. So far, we have spoken of cosmic evil, of evil as it is found in nature, of suffering, death, disease, or even of old age, or of the explosion of galaxies — a thing which was unknown and inconceivable to Maimonides — as though annihilation is lurking around the corner, awaiting everything in the universe.

There is, however, another kind of evil, the evil which exists within man himself. If we have described the first type of evil as cosmic evil, we can describe the second one as anthropological evil. Thus, in practice we return into the depths of the human soul in search of this anthropological evil, of whose existence we have only hinted so far.

Maimonides speaks of Sammael, and in Book 2, Chapter 22 of *Guide to the Perplexed*, he refers to a number of midrashim which are bound together. One must admit that understanding Maimonides' words on this issue involves us in some interesting quandaries of modern research, to which we shall hint in what follows. Maimonides was always perplexed by alternatives. In one way, he did not want to present the principles of his doctrine before the multitude, knowing that his doctrine would not be properly understood, and that many people would be misled by it. Philosophy, which is apparently the crown of human achievement, is also an extremely dangerous science. It does not only supply us with meaning and significance — it can also mislead people and make them stray from the direct road.

When Maimonides was faced with his great discoveries in Biblical exegesis and his new understanding of the secrets of the Bible and of Talmudic literature, he did not, on the one hand, wish to deprive the reader of the possibility of comprehending these secrets. But on the other hand, he did not want to expound these secrets to everyone. He therefore chose a very individual and interesting fashion which consists of concealing and revealing at the same time.

Thus, Maimonides brings before us Talmudic aggadot and hints at a certain solution, but the solution, in accordance with his method, is to be found in an entirely different passage, and it is for this solution which we must look.

In Book 3, Chapter 22, Maimonides refers to the evil inclination in man, which is Satan, and cites an interesting legend which asserts that each man is accompanied by two angels, one on his right side and one on his left, and these are the good inclination and the evil inclination. This legend is well-known to many readers in one or another of its versions. Especially well-known is the version which tells us that a good angel and an evil angel accompany each man on his way back home from synagogue on the eve of the Sabbath. When the table is laid and everything is ready for the celebration of the Sabbath, the good angel makes a blessing and the bad angel is

56

forced, against his will, to say Amen, and — God forbid — the other way around.

This aggadah appears in a great number of versions, but what is most interesting is that Maimonides' version does not appear anywhere. In one of my studies, where I searched for the Talmudic source of that legend, I pointed out an interesting fact which had not been noticed before, since most of us are accustomed to read the text of the *Guide to the Perplexed* in the Hebrew translation. But Maimonides wrote his book in Arabic, and in this passage — written, of course in Arabic — he said that there are two angels, one to a man's right and one to his left. But here he added *in Hebrew*: "and these are the good inclination and the bad inclination." Thus, Maimonides did not create here a legend which had not existed before, but he interpolated his own comment into an existing legend. But why do this? I believe — and this is the thesis I developed in that study — that Maimonides used the Hebrew word for "left," SMOL, in order to explain to us the etymology of the name SAMMAEL. This involves only a change of one letter in Hebrew.

Who is Sammael, or Satan? At first sight, we all know the answer to this question. Satan is a force outside us which tempts us and enjoys the doing of evil deeds. He is the deceiver, a force which makes us stray from the way of righteousness. But the truth is that Sammael is not outside us, but rather — as Maimonides makes it virtually clear — is merely our left side, using the term "left" in the well-known symbolic sense, where right and left designate good and evil.

Thus, Sammael is not a cosmic entity which enters us from without, but an entity which is to be found inside us, within man himself. That is, in man himself there is a good force and evil force. Maimonides, probably on the basis of his readings in other sources, identifies Sammael with the imagination. Thus, he writes in Book 2, Chapter 6: "All this follows in the steps of the imagination, which is the real evil inclination: for every lack of this thing is a lack in beliefs, and the influence of the imagination continues even after the action."

As we have seen in one of the previous chapters, Maimonides noted that there is an internal struggle going on in each man, a struggle between the imagination and reason, between good and evil. Imagination is the factor which draws man toward evil, and thus it is the very Sammael of whom the Talmudic Sages spoke.

This brings us to one of the most interesting and fascinating issues in the whole of this field, the story of the Garden of Eden. The story of the Garden of Eden has always been a constant source of speculation for all religious thinkers. The truth is that there is a great enigma implied in any attempt to understand this story — even at its face value. Let us raise only one central question: why are Adam and Eve forbidden to eat the fruits of the tree? If we observe the answers given by various thinkers, even a partial survey — and I emphasize that I am only dealing with a partial survey — will show that there are, essentially, two approaches which contradict each other. On the one hand, one can understand this story as if it was a pagan myth —and some modern scholars have, indeed, attempted to understand it as such. Here we have God in possession of a tree with some wonderful magical qualities, and in His jealousy, he does not allow man an access to it. This *motif* is very frequent in Greek mythology, and the classic example is the myth of Prometheus. Prometheus stole fire from the gods, who refused to give it to man, thus imparting to man the power and the ability to develop technology and industry. Prometheus is a benefactor of the human race, a symbol of the struggle of a Titan against the gods in order to improve the state of man. To many scholars, he is the embodiment of a teacher who teaches many kinds of knowledge. The Marxist approach, for example, sees in him a hero who symbolizes, by his very revolt against the gods, some of its own doctrines and beliefs. In a similar fashion, one can approach the story of the Garden of Eden, and conceive of the tree of knowledge, and of wisdom, as something which the gods begrudged man, and man's eating of the forbidden fruit as the act of the heroic Titan. This is one approach.

On the other hand, there are thinkers who accept this interpretation in principle, but discover in this story God's mercy rather than His jealousy. After all, what is the source of our suffering and of evil? The source of evil is nothing but knowledge, for the man who increases his knowledge increases his pain. Here we see man in paradise — one might almost say, in a fool's paradise. It is wisdom and knowledge which will take him out of this paradise — especially the most vital knowledge: man's knowledge that he will die.

Thus it transpires that knowledge is far from being the good thing which Prometheus assumed it to be. On the contrary. We know, therefore we suffer. This is an idea which is also expressed in *Avot of Rabbi Nathan*, and is close to the myth of Pandora's Box — as though God wanted to deprive us of knowledge, of the use of our reason, and because we sinned we are condemned to suffer from it. This is an exegesis which is opposed to the previous one, but at the same time it shares the same basis, since it regards the tree of knowledge of good and evil as a tree which imparted wisdom to us.

But there are other interpretations. No doubt, the sexual interpretation offers itself in connection with the tree of *knowledge* and with Adam who *knew* Eve his wife. But Maimonides, followed by most of the Jewish philosophical interpreters, did not choose any of these ways of exegesis. Maimonides could not have accepted the Prometheus-type interpretation, since it would entail what, to him, would be an absurdity. On the other hand, Maimonides and other Jewish commentators were fully aware that God's image in man is reason. Man is human only because he has knowledge and wisdom, only on account of his reason. This is God's image in man. Thus, it is impossible to conceive of man as a creature whom God defends against wisdom. Man could not even accept, or understand, a commandment like "You shall not eat," if he was not endowed with reason.

This is the human point in Maimonides' exegesis. We cannot accept a thesis which maintains that knowledge is the result of a transgression or a sin, since this would be absurd. This seems to Maimonides to be non-Jewish, incorrect, and out of tune with a precise interpretation of the Bible. Here, Maimonides draws our attention to the interesting fact that nowhere in the Bible do we find "a tree of knowledge of truth and falsehood," but only "a tree of knowledge of good and evil." We, who have been studying this issue of good and evil in an attempt to reach beneath the surface, realize immediately that this is a vast difference. For what we have here is not human reason, attempting to reach the truth at any price, but a different area, an area which was sealed before man until he sinned, and was now laid open before him. The fundamental proof of this interpretation is that the first act of Adam and Eve after this sin is connected with their feeling of shame. They have now learned what shame is. They feel, they know, they open their eyes and see that they are naked, and they make themselves garments out of fig-leaves. This implies that man has now come into the possession of another area of knowledge; he has now penetrated into that problematic area of good and evil.

This basic intuition of Maimonides is unusually fruitful. There is little doubt that it embodies much of the truth, even as far as the simple interpretation of the Biblical story is concerned. But it is open to many possibilities of interpretation and of understanding even as far as its own meaning is concerned. For Maimonides reads the Biblical story in an allegorical fashion. I shall mention two possibilities of interpreting Maimonides' words: the first is interesting on account of its simplicity and beauty, and the second seems to me to be more important because it is closer to Maimonides' own words and to ideas which developed under their influence.

I shall bring an example of the first of these two interpretations from a popular book which is fundamentally midrashic — *Nivei Zahav* by Rabbi Ze'ev Gold. Rabbi Gold maintains that before this sin, man was in possession of objective knowledge, whereas after his sin, he fell into the subjective world. The truth is that we cannot conceive of reality as it is. We cannot reach the truth in various fields — and a comparison between a series of lectures, say, in mathematics and a series of lectures in philosophy or politics will provide a good example of this.

The question of good and evil is thus not an external issue, in the sense I have just explained. It is inside me and I am involved in it. I have eaten of the tree of knowledge of good and evil, and now I distort reality. Reality itself is no longer seen in the right way. I remember a rabbi in an ethically-inclined yeshivah teaching his pupils this fact by example. He took a small coin and put it in front of a pupil's eye, covering his other eye with his hand. Then he said: "You can now learn how a small coin near your eye conceals from you a large man who is far from you." A coin which is close to us sometimes prevents us from noticing other people. It is, in fact, the problem of subjectivity and of the many interests we have. We are conscious of some of these interests, but we are unaware of many of them, and thus we do not know how and why we distort reality. This, according to the interpretation I have just given, is the significance of the tree of knowledge of good and evil and of man's eating of its fruit.

But Maimonides seems to approach it in a far more complex manner, involving an interesting set of symbols. He cites a legend from *Pirkei de-Rabbi Eliezer*, an interesting and bizarre story, in which the snake appears as some sort of camel, whose rider is Sammael himself. Thus, there is one hero in this legend who is never mentioned in the Bible — Sammael. Who is this Sammael? We have already seen that Sammael, for Maimonides, is probably our faculty of imagination. Thus there is a conflict within man, a war between good and evil; between his imagination, which allows him to eat of the fruit of the tree of knowledge, promising to make him like God in his knowledge of good and evil, and God's command.

It is true that, in his reaction to Adam's sin, God says (Genesis 3:22): "Behold, the man is become as one of us, to know good and evil." It is as though God agreed with the words of the snake. But on my reading of Maimonides' exegesis, this is only irony on the part of God. God utters these words in an ironical manner, in the language of ridicule. This idea was already familiar to the Biblical commentators of the Middle Ages, and two them, Rabbi Hillel of Verona and Don Isaac Abarbanel, expressed it in their writings. The gist of it is that the imaginative faculty deceives man by promising him something which it will not, and cannot, fulfill.

Sammael and the snake seem to fulfill the same function in the legend we have discussed. But according to Abarbanel, the snake signifies man's will. Thus we have, on the one hand, imagination and the will, the former influencing the latter. On the other hand, we have the Cherubim, guarding the way of the tree of life. The story will be incomplete if we do not see it as a struggle between two kinds of angels. On the one hand, we have Sammael, who is himself an angel, and on the other, the Cherubim, with the sword which guards the way to the tree of life.

Medieval philosophical exegesis has a little surprise for us on this point. We usually take it that the Cherubim guard the tree of life in order to prevent us from reaching it. The interpretation I am about to expound will look rather strange. But the reader should remember that in the Temple there was the Ark of the Covenant, and on it there were engraved two Cherubim. In the Ark was the scroll of the Torah, the Torah of which it is written (Proverbs 3,18) "She is a tree of life to them that lay hold upon her." Maimonides, therefore, saw in the story of the tree of life the secret of man's final aim. Adam's story is not a story of something which happened in the past, but the story of each of us at every moment and in every single person's life. There is a war inside each of us — between imagination on the one hand, and on the other hand, our intellectual and rational powers, which want man to eat of the tree of life. What is this tree of life? In this context, it is taken to mean the most sublime state which man can reach, a state which Maimonides and other famous thinkers in the following generations described as *dvekut* (devotion). If you wish, you can understand this term to imply man's capacity to reach beyond himself into the spiritual and transcendental world. Devotion is the option man has of emerging beyond his limitations.

I would like to end our discussion of this legend on a modern note, which I owe to a remark of one of my pupils. The Cherubim guard the way to the garden of Eden, but they also have a flaming sword, which is a symbol of the drugs men often use in an attempt to reach beyond themselves and arrive at something transcendent. Thus, man has before him a dazzling light which can spellbind him and mislead him, but this is only the light of a flaming sword, a sword which gives man death, not life.

Maimonides read in an allegorical fashion not only the story of the tree of life, as a struggle between Satan, or Sammael, and the Cherubim. He also interpreted allegorically the sequel to this episode, the story of Cain and Abel.

Cain and Abel embody two types of life which epitomize the fullest development of human potential in man before he has reached his rational level. Maimonides refers here to the legend which says that before Adam begat his third son, Seth, his children for 130 years were demons. For Maimonides, there is no doubt that the demons mentioned in this legend are none but Cain and Abel. Both Cain and Abel stand, for Maimonides, as symbols of types of life which have not reached their full perfection. This is the meaning of demons. For what, after all, is a demon? A demon is created when reason and thought, which are devised for protecting man's perfection, are exploited by all sorts of devices which produce evil consequences. Thus, Maimonides sees the existence of demons as the most widespread sort of existence, the existence of human beings who are endowed with reason, but use their reason for evil purposes. Thus, a demonic existence is that of Abel, who — as one of Maimonides' commentators remarks — stands for the fool, or for foolishness. But Cain, too, stands for man who had arrived at many technological achievements, but the purpose of these achievements is evil. When this evil predominates, it becomes the source of murder and war. These are the devices of human reason when used for evil purposes.

Sammael, our power of imagination, which we saw in the previous story, is now bent on the production of demons. He now gives birth to a human being endowed with a power which he uses in the wrong manner. This unbridled force of evil turns into the source of wickedness and crime. This is the unbridled demon, who destroys everything he meets on his way — the demon who no longer knows how to keep his brother.

VII.

Good and Evil in
the Kabbalah

So far, we have traced the attitude of philosophy — especially that
of Maimonides — to the problem of evil. We have also seen some of
the projections of this philosophy on a later generation. We have
mentioned Leibniz, and Voltaire's ridicule of Leibniz in the form of
the confirmed optimist, Candide, who believes that our world is the
best of all possible worlds.

We have explained how Rabbi Abraham Isaac Kook regarded
this philosophical position not as an optimistic one, but rather as a
pessimistic view. In Part 2 of *Orot ha-Kodesh*, Rabbi Kook speaks
of "the profundity of good and the profundity of evil," a pair of
concepts which he borrowed from that ancient and mysterious
book, *Sefer Yetzirah*, in which the Kabbalists saw their basic book.
Rabbi Kook writes:

> The Wisdom of Mysteries (that is, the Kabbalah) explains
> the reality of the spiritual dimension with all its values. It
> interprets being in the fullness of its character. It expounds
> good and evil to their full extent.

Rabbi Kook, who regards himself as a disciple of the wisdom of
the Kabbalah and its exegete to the twentieth century, goes on to say
that the profundity of good encircles the profundity of evil; that
there is a profundity of evil, but that it has its roots in good. He
adds: "And for this reason, there is in the whole universe a reality of
the desire for evil, both moral evil and practical evil." Rabbi Kook is
thus maintaining that evil is no illusion but a reality. There is,

64

indeed, an inclination for evil: "The desire for the destruction of the world exists in reality for all its values, just as there exists the desire for its construction, elevation and improvement."

In a surprising manner, one can find here parallels to some aspects of the psychological system of Sigmund Freud. In the earlier stages of Freud's psychology, we witnessed his attempt to explain everything on the basis of the principle of pleasure in its various transformations. But the First World War revealed to him that it would be insufficient to explain everything in the world on the basis of this pleasure principle alone. Freud then discovered the other principle, which he called Thanatos — death, or evil. Something very similar is said here by Rabbi Kook.

Beside the positive desire for the improvement of the world and its elevation, there is also the desire for the destruction of the world, and this desire is real, and exists in all areas and all spheres. The force of evil is thus not merely a privation as Maimonides thought, not a mere zero or negation. It exists beside what we have described, in algebraic terms, as A. Minus A (-A) is a force which exists side by side with it. This is a limiting and opposing force, which finds its expression in the world at large and in man's destructive instinct, his instinct of self-annihilation.

We shall return later to Rabbi Kook's thought and observe the consequences of this fact of the positive existence of evil and his interpretation of it. What matters at the moment is that here, in these few sentences, one is able to epitomize the great message of the Kabbalistic doctrine of evil in the interpretation given it by Rabbi Kook — that good and evil are present to us as two parallel principles, as A and -A, which are both existent.

Without entering into details of the literature of the Kabbalah, one should remark that we have, by and large, two types of Kabbalistic literature, as far as our problem is concerned. There are texts which employ a philosophical, abstract and theoretical language, but there are other texts which speak the language of aggadah and imagery which is close to myth. This makes this type of aggadic literature of great interest and fascination. If we have, so far, emphasized the conceptual treatment of our problem, we shall now lay stress on a completely different attitude, an attitude which includes numerous artistic and literary elements.

In the nature of the subject, we shall have to make this survey brief and schematic. I shall rely on Professor Isaiah Tishbi's *Mishnat ha-Zohar*, Volume 1, to which I refer the reader for more information. As an introductory note, one should remark that it is impossible to speak of one Kabbalistic view, since the Kabbalah includes many streams, and stretches over long periods. I shall not enter here into problems of the development of the Kabbalah. Instead, I shall present the reader with a number of models used in the Kabbalah for depicting good and evil and their relations.

Let us turn to the first of these models, which I shall call the model of right and left. There are, in the upper world of the ten *sefirot* (emanations), *hesed* (mercy, or love) and *gevurah* (power or force), as well as *middat ha-rahamim* and *middat ha-din* (the divine attribute of mercy and the divine attribute of judgment). This classification continues a thread of thought which is already found in the literature of the Talmudic Sages, according to which there are two divine *middot* (literally, "measures": qualities or attributes) in the world. The quality of mercy and the quality of judgment are conceived here as struggling, or arguing, between themselves, as personifications of a cosmic prosecutor and a cosmic defender. On the one hand, we have love and bounty, and on the other, we have power and force — the realization that this bounty must be restricted, even in the interest of its recipient. These, then, are the emanations of *hesed* and *gevurah*, which should be brought to a synthesis which is called, in the Kabbalah, *tiferet* (glory). This duality between God's bounty and its limitation is described in the symbolism of the Kabbalah by means of right and left, just like the two hands of a human being. One remembers the Talmudic expression, "the right hand accepts and the left hand rejects." In a similar manner, we have two forces, bounty and power, on the metaphysical level.

What is the origin of evil? Evil is created in the sphere of power, in the quality of judgment. It is the consequence of the need of a quality of judgment, and we feel it in the same way that the son feels evil when his father punishes him. This continues the classic thread of thought, which regards evil as a punishment — but there is an interesting addition here. The Kabbalah believes that man is a small world, a reproduction, on a smaller scale, of cosmic reality. Just as there is right and left, bounty and power, above, so there are also in man right and left, or two inclinations, the good inclination and the evil inclination. Cosmic good and evil are thus paralleled by the good and evil inside man. And since there is this parallelism, when a man activates the evil principle within himself, he also sets in motion the cosmic evil outside him.

I would like to explain things, at this stage, by means of three scenes in a puppet theater, which will make the first model we find in the Kabbalah more graphic and concrete. In one of the previous chapters, we spoke of the pagan view which maintains that man is bound by the fetters of fate, that he is in the power of superior forces, whose course he is unable to change. In our first scene, we witness the puppets tied by strings above them. They move their limbs only because someone above them pulls the strings. This is precisely the picture which corresponds to pagan fatalism, which maintains that man has no power to change anything. Man is, as it were, part of a cosmic theater, but the truth is that he is merely a figure in this theater, a puppet which is moved by someone else.

Against this background, let us now consider the Biblical revolution and depict it by a second scene in our theater. We are still in the same puppet theater; but now we have cut the strings and set the puppets free — or set man free. But now we are already in a completely different kind of theater. This is the theater which Maimonides depicted for us when he maintained that there are, indeed, superior forces, but man is still capable of being the architect of his destiny, playing his part in the theater, in a play the scenario of which is not wholly given to him. The last word has not yet been said. There is a general outline. We know that the end must be good — an end which will constitute salvation — but we are free, and it is up to us to bring this play to its end.

In the Kabbalah, we are faced with a third kind of scene. At first sight, we are back in the puppet theater. The puppets are once more tied by strings. But the situation has now been reversed — for it is now the puppets who are pulling the strings. We have here something of a fundamental rebellion. The puppet has acquired its own personality, as it were, and is now taking over from those who were activating it. This is the Kabbalistic idea, and, in contrast to Maimonides' view, it aimed at giving man stupendous powers. Man has now assumed cosmic dimensions, for by his personal behavior he changes the world. He has now become, in a new shape, the center of the universe, being tied with strings which move the forces above, the same forces which, in the past, were regarded as moving him. This is the first model we find in the Kabbalah, according to which man, in his activities, his actions, and his choice between bounty and power, changes cosmic reality.

In this situation, I can bestow the good which is in me on the world, and we thus have a correspondence between the small world and the large world, which are bound together by the bonds of bounty, or emanation. So much for our first model, which we have called the model of right and left.

But when we turn to the Book of Zohar, we find, beside this model, another model as well, which depicts evil as "The Other Side" (*sitra ahara*). Here, we no longer have left and right as two integral sides of the same thing, but two sides which are totally different from each other, producing a symmetry between good and evil.

What does this model teach us? We recall here the words of Rabbi Kook, that evil, too, has its own structure; that it is no mere accident; that it does not consist of isolated phenomena, of which you could say that these are insignificant occurrences. Far from it. Evil has its own structure. It appears as "The Other Side," as possessing a structure which corresponds to the structure of the good, having its own emanations, just as there are emanations in holiness. This is no longer a model of right and left as we have seen previously, in which the excess of left, designating evil, is seen merely like a father punishing or tormenting his children, thus turning the quality of judgment into evil. Here we are faced with an entirely different phenomenon.

In holiness, just as in unholiness, there are now left and right. There are a male element and a female element in holiness, just as much as they exist in unholiness, and these are parallel structures. I have emphasized this point of the male and female elements since, despite the similarities, it is fundamentally different from a modern dualist position which the reader might have encountered in the recent play, *A Jewish Soul*. This play represents a particular Jewish thinker, Otto Weininger, who has had something of a revival in recent years. Weininger attempted to depict the world as the theater of war between two forces, good and evil, where good is the male element and evil is the female element. The Jews belong, of course, to the realm of evil, since they are effeminate and female. The consequence which Weininger drew from this is that the Jew has nothing left for him but to commit suicide. It was no accident that this was the only book written by a Jew which was allowed by Hitler to occupy a place of honor in respectable libraries of the Third Reich.

There is the most profound difference between this view and the Kabbalistic model we are now discussing. In the Kabbalah, we have seen that both good and evil have their structure, and that both contain a male element, *yesod*, and a female element, *malkhut* ("foundation" and "kingdom" respectively — the first of these words is masculine in Hebrew, the second is feminine). The feminine side is embodied, for example, in the fact that God has a "presence" (*shekhinah* — another feminine Hebrew word). Thus, just as we speak of God as "He," we should also speak of Him in the feminine gender — which is why His presence, the *shekhinah*, is depicted in the Kabbalah in the form of a woman. But the "Other Side," too, has its good and evil, and the good and evil on "The Other Side" are depicted by the figures of Ashmedai and Lillith, who represent the masculine and the feminine aspects of "The Other Side." It is interesting to note that the Zohar explains many events which occur in this world as the influence of the masculine or feminine aspects of "The Other Side."

We are thus faced with two forces which confront each other. Just as there are, in holiness, "crowns of faith," so there are in unholiness "crowns of magic." In holiness, there are seven constructive emanations, in unholiness there are seven vanities — the vanities which are mentioned in Ecclesiastes' "vanity of vanities." In holiness, there are ten emanations, and in unholiness there are ten crocodiles lying on the shores of ten great rivers, which correspond to the ten commands with which God created the world. This model of "The Other Side," *sitra ahara*, has had considerable influence, and it has become an ordinary idiom in present-day Hebrew. We shall discuss its uses in modern Hebrew later to remember the attitude of the philosophers to Rabbi Abbahu's legend, that God created worlds and destroyed them. These worlds, it appeared, were the possibilities which were rejected; they were those worlds might have existed, but were destroyed.

The third model which I wish to discuss is what one can call the model of refuse. It is interesting as being less perfect than our world. In the Kabbalah, on the other hand, these worlds exist in reality and in the midst of us. They are not unrealized possibilities, but even they, the rejected possibilities, have some degree of reality. These destroyed worlds exist here and now, and the Zohar describes them in many different shapes and forms. It speaks of our world as containing "the dirt of judgment" and "the dregs of the wine." The Zohar maintains that our world is a world where there is not only wine, but also the dregs; not only gold, but melted gold, gold dust, gold alloy and dross. If there is judgment, there is also refuse. It is, indeed, a world which appears to be good, and it is true that it is the best of all possible worlds. But this world also has its other sides. The description of the world as good cannot be definitive, since we must realize that the Other Side is also real, and this is the evil against which we must struggle.

Let us now consider some of the Kabbalistic characterizations of the relations between good and evil. These characterizations mainly suit our second model, that of the Other Side. The Zohar depicts reality as a war between good and evil. We can no longer think here in terms of a tree which casts a shadow, as the philosophers did. What we have here is a war between two forces — the force of holiness and the force of unholiness, the Good Side and the Other Side.

The Other Side, *sitra ahara*, is depicted here in the image of "other gods." When the Bible commands us "You shall not have other gods," this does not only mean that we should not believe in idols. In a more profound sense, it means that we should not make a covenant with the Devil and yield to evil. The evil inclination is not merely "man's left side" — it is the representative of the Other Side which is embedded in man. This is the source of the desire for the destruction of the world and for our own annihilation, which Freud revealed to us. We can now regard in a different manner the same intuition which we have seen here. It is an inclination for destruction which is directed, not only toward others, but toward one's own self.

Evil, in the Kabbalah, is symbolized by the snake. We remember that, for Maimonides, evil was Sammael riding on the snake. Here, evil is the snake itself. One example which might explain to us the nature of the new options open to us when we pass from the realm of philosophy to the realm of Kabbalah, is the interpretation of a well-known verse on the Book of Psalms (81:9), which every Jew says in his morning prayers on Thursdays: "There shall no strange god be in you." Its simple sense is clear: there should be no other god in the Congregation of Israel.

But already the Talmudic Sages interpreted this verse in an entirely different sense. "In you," they said, does not refer to the community, or the congregation, but to what is within you. What could be the strange god within you? The evil inclination, of course. This is a midrashic exegesis, whose aim is to arouse man to struggle against his evil inclination.

How did the philosophers interpret this verseT Let us first cite an example ascribed to the Jewish scholar in nineteenth-century Frankfurt, Rabbi Samson Raphael Hirsch. Rabbi Hirsch had an admirer, who later became more famous than the rabbi — Heinrich Graetz, the author of the monumental *History of the Jews*. When Graetz was young, he wrote a book about Jewish Gnosticism, which was also well known to Rabbi Samson Raphael Hirsch. Hirsch

71

interprets the verse of the Psalms, "There shall no strange god be in you" in the following sense: "Do not think that the evil inclination within you is a god." Thus, Hirsch takes the Talmudic midrash and understands it as part of the struggle against Gnosticism. But the Kabbalah understood it differently. It said simply that "There shall no strange god be in you" implies precisely that there *is* a strange god within you. True, this is not a god in the proper significance of "the Infinite;" but there is still within you a strange force, and you have to struggle against this strange force. There is within us, as it were, a struggle between two powers, pulling in two different directions.

In Maimonides' thought, we met with an attempt to explain good and evil in immanent, internal terms. Sammael has turned into *smol*, left —that is, he is no longer an external entity, but he is within you. In the Kabbalah, we see this internal force being externalized. The evil inclination which is within you has become the envoy of a far greater force, of the force of evil which exists in the whole cosmos, and in the name of which it struggles. It is, as it were, the force of chaos, of the void, of crocodiles fighting against the very act of creation.

Thus we are faced once again with a dualism. This is not exactly a Gnostic dualism. There is, in the history of the Kabbalah, an interesting phenomenon discovered by the experts and explained in detail by Professor Tishbi in the introduction to the book I mentioned at the beginning of this chapter. There were, indeed, some Kabbalists who were perhaps inclined toward Gnosticism, and there was a whole Kabbalistic school of this sort in the town of Burgos in Castillia. But in the main stream of the Kabbalah, things are different. The Kabbalah recognizes the existence of a struggle between good and evil, but this is still far from a Gnostic view, since both good and evil are messengers of the same one God. They symbolize for us a battle, for the consequences of which we alone are responsible, since we alone are able to win this battle.

VIII.

The Doctrine of Kelippot *and Pacifism*

In the last chapter, we delineated three models of good and evil in the Kabbalah, the chief of which is called the model of The Other Side, the *sitra ahara*. Now I wish to present you with another model which can be found in the Kabbalah, and which has a crucial importance for the later development of Jewish thought, as well as being a term which has penetrated into everyday Hebrew.

I refer to the model of *kelippot* (shells), to which the model of *nitzotzot* (sparks) corresponds to some degree. Let us observe this model — by our reckoning, the fourth Kabbalistic model. This model of the shells is based on a verse from the Book of Ezekiel. When the prophet Ezekiel sees the famous vision of the chariot of God, he notes (Ezekiel 1:4): "...a whirlwind came out of the north, a great cloud, and a fire infolding itself, and a brightness was about it, and out of the midst thereof as the color of amber, out of the midst of the fire."

This vision of the most sublime holiness, which includes fire and amber, was conceived in the Kabbalah as surrounded by four shells, as it were: the first shell is the whirlwind, the second is the great cloud, the third, the fire infolding itself, and the fourth, a brightness about it. This is to say that, when holiness is revealed, it is surrounded by shells. The Kabbalah made use of this idea to maintain that holiness always appears to us in the same manner, like the core of a nut surrounded by shells. These shells are evil.

Beside this conception, we meet with another doctrine which

was developed in the later stage of the Kabbalah, at the stage known as Lurianic Kabbalah, the Kabbalah of Rabbi Isaac Luria, which flourished in Safed in the sixteenth century. Lurianic Kabbalah has a doctrine of sparks — the sparks of holiness scattered in the world — and the core of this doctrine is the idea that there can be sparks of good within evil itself. It appears that if we were to amalgamate these two doctrines, we could reach the conclusion that what they have in common is the idea that good and evil are intermixed, so that one cannot find pure good, just as one cannot find pure evil — evil which one would wish to reject in its entirety.

Sometimes, evil is tied up with good like a shell, and sometimes, in a different manner, good is to be found within evil. We are thus surprised to find, in the realm of Jewish mysticism, ideas which were later developed in modern existentialist thought, and which spoke of an intermixture of good and evil. In the light of this idea, man's eating of the fruit of the tree of knowledge of good and evil is interpreted as an act which is characteristic of our existence, in which everything is a mixture of good and evil. Against the background of such an existence, salvation will be that state of affairs in which we will be able to separate good from evil. This idea sounds abstract and symbolic, but we shall soon see, by examining some concrete examples from the writings of modern and recent thinkers, how far this problem of separating and distinguishing good from evil is an acute and difficult contemporary issue.

I shall start, therefore, with the position of some modern thinkers on this issue — modern thinkers who are fully aware of this Kabbalistic symbolism. Chief among them is the American Jewish thinker Abraham Joshua Heschel, one of the greatest champions of human rights —the rights of Jews as well as the rights of blacks in the United States. Heschel conducted a permanent dialogue with American theology, and in one of his articles, published in his book *The Insecurity of Freedom*, he discussed the problem of the mixture of good and evil. This mixture has many dimensions. I shall cite only two simple examples. The first is presented by Heschel himself in the name of Rabbi Jacob Joseph of

Polonnoye, a pupil of Rabbi Israel Baal Shem Tov, the founder of the Hasidic movement.

On the verse (Eccl. 7:20) "For there is not a just man upon earth, that does good, and sins not," the Baal Shem Tov said that, at first glance, this appears to depict a well-known state of affairs. None of us is pure and perfect, none of us is completely righteous. Each of us is prone to failure and sin. But the Biblical verse speaks of the *just*; "There is no just man upon earth, that does good, and sins not." The Baal Shem Tov himself interpreted this verse to mean "there is no just man upon earth who does good." That is, he maintains, that even in the good act of a just man, there is an admixture of evil. He raises the question of whether the good act is done for its own sake, without an ulterior motive, or whether there is some reason other than the good itself for the performance of a good act.

Be that as it may, this interpretation of our verse assumes that even within the good act there is evil. In fact, we can never do good — as Rabbi Jacob Joseph tells us in the name of the Baal Shem Tov.

This story embodies, in the most pessimistic manner, the fact that always, even when we perform the most altruistic acts, there is an admixture of some egoistic element in each thing which we do. This may be the meaning of the Talmudic saying (B. *Sukkah* 52a) that "The greater a man is, the greater his evil inclination." That is, good and evil accompany us at every stage of our development.

In order to give an example of the problems involved in the assumption of these *kelippot* — the shells — I shall make use of a discussion which is almost contemporary. It comes from the early years of the present century, but the problems it deals with are, unfortunately, still with us today. I shall start with introducing the reader to the author of these views, a figure who — and I say this with much sadness — is hardly known to the Jewish reader today: Aaron Samuel Tomrat. Tomrat was an Eastern European rabbi, who was at first a follower of Zionism, and even a delegate to the Fourth Zionist Congress, but later left it. He wrote a series of books, signing them with the literary name "One of the Rabbis who Feel." They include such titles as *Judaism and Liberty* (1905), *Torah*

Ethics and Judaism (1912), and, later, *The Congregation of Israel and the War of the Gentiles.*

To put it simply, Rabbi Tomrat was a pacifist. He was the representative of pacifism in modern Jewish thought, and he conducted a major struggle against the ideology which finds justifications for war. In a nutshell, he maintained that there are two kinds of corruption —corruption originating in the body, and corruption originating in the mind. Corruption of the body occurs when people are engaged in plain murder, without any excuses or pretexts for the perpetration of this murder. This is plain corruption. But there is another kind of corruption, which consists of wicked actions originating in "the naughty intellect" — "naughty," not in the usual sense of this word, but rather in the sense of "wayward" — an intellect which has strayed from the direct path and is trying to make others stray from it.

Sometimes, we have massacres and persecutions which don the garb of theology and ideology. Rabbi Tomrat gives as examples the massacres and the persecutions of the Jews at the hands of the gentiles, which have been going on for thousands of years, on the pretext that they are perpetrated because the Jews refuse to worship the gentiles' deities. But another example — and this is an interesting point — is the persecutions carried out by the so-called righteous within Israel, who persecute their own brethren in the name of the worship of God.

These are wicked persecutions, supported by a cunning pretext. For example, it is clear to an outside observer that slavery is an absurdity, which has no right to exist. But, in order to keep the institution of slavery, people created an ideology which made it permissible for one person to be the master of another. This found its practical expression, in the words of Rabbi Tomrat, in the fact

> that they attempted, at first, to keep their slaves in darkness and ignorance, so as to have a pretext for dominating them, since they could point their finger at their low estate and explain that they should, in accordance with it, be bridled like cattle. Rabbi Tomrat, who died in 1931, witnessed the First World

War, but not the Second. It is interesting to read his following words:

> With such great force did Germany send out thousands of her sons to the slaughter. This was the elemental force of the majority, while the rest stood aside indifferently. What is more, they sang the praises of this pestilential war with songs of praise and patriotic hymns, with such force that even the victims themselves felt only the pain, but not the injustice and deception inflicted on them.

Rabbi Tomrat is implying here that ideology deprives a man of his sense of injustice and leaves him only with his feelings of pain. It takes away from him the ability to discern evil wherever it exists.

His view of ideology is summed up by Rabbi Tomrat in reference to the story of the exodus from Egypt. Here, he conceives of the problem in its concrete embodiment — one might say, in its political embodiment.

In interpreting the familiar words of the Passover Haggadah, "And I shall pass through the land of Egypt — I, not a messenger," Rabbi Tomrat writes that the exodus from Egypt was performed by God himself, who struck the Egyptians and took out the children of Israel, and even the act of revenge was performed by God himself, not by a human agency "In order that the persecuted would not turn, at the moment of their liberation, into persecutors."

Let us now compare Tomrat's interpretation of this with the Talmudic aggadah, B. *Baba Kama* 60a: "And none of you shall go out at the door of his house until the morning" (Exodus 12:22). Why was it forbidden for them to come out while the plague was being inflicted? "Because, once the slaughterer has been given a free hand, he does not distinguish between the righteous and the wicked."

On the face of it, this is a mythical imagery familiar to us from the various Kabbalistic conceptions. It appears that Satan, or The Other Side, who no longer knows the distinction between good and evil, is at large here. If the Children of Israel were outside their houses on that day, the plague would have killed them all. But Rabbi Tomrat interprets this idea in a surprising manner. "The slaughterer" of the Talmudic legend is not the Angel of Death, but

77

the slaughterer within each man. If you make use of the sword — this is what Rabbi Tomrat learns from the story — you no longer distinguish the righteous from the wicked. Once the slaughterer has been let loose, once people have been allowed to use the sword, the distinction between just and unjust men is no longer there, and the defender will, of necessity, turn into aggressor. There is no other possibility.

The Biblical commandment never to return to Egypt is thus understood in the sense that, once we have attained our independent life, we should not introduce into it the confidence in brute force which characterized the Egyptians. It is for this reason that the king of Israel (Deut. 17:18) "...shall not multiply horses to himself, so that he may not cause the people to return to Egypt."

This is, therefore, the view of a man who had learned from observation that one cannot make a clear distinction between the shells and the sparks, between good and evil. Having seen that in practical life it is extremely difficult to make this distinction, he drew the conclusion and arrived at total pacifism.

As against this conclusion, I would like to cite the reaction of a contemporary of Rabbi Tomrat, Rabbi Abraham Isaac Kook. When Rabbi Kook writes about war — the activity which was totally rejected by Tomrat — he says: "And as to the matter of wars, it was utterly impossible, while all their neighbors were like wolves, that the people of Israel alone would not fight." One expects, at some future date, "mankind as it should be. But one should not anticipate."

These words of Rabbi Kook make one feel that real life, or reality, are such that, within them, it is impossible to draw a clear distinction between good and evil, and that sometimes, because of one's desire to realize the purposes of good, he must employ evil means. This brings us to an interesting and important issue, which one might call the problem of contradiction. When we observe the thought of Rabbi Kook, a man who always attempted to overcome contradiction, as well as the ideas of some other thinkers, we shall detect four contradictions which perplex moral thought. In order to make this more concrete, I will call them by allegorical names. The

78

first of these contradictions is the contradiction of the serpent, or the snake. There is one fact which must be clear to us — that this world is no longer a paradise full of harmony, and the symbol of this state of affairs is the snake, of whom it is written (Gen. 3:15): "And I will put enmity between you and the woman, and between your seed and her seed."

We are at war with the serpent, a struggle we cannot always be free from. But there is also another struggle which we have encountered again and again in the past, and this is symbolized by the words (Gen. 4:7) "Sin lies at the door." Evil is found, not only outside us, in the form of the snake, but also inside us. Let us observe the comment of *Rashi* on the verse in Genesis in which God tells Cain that "sin lies at the door." *Rashi* writes: "And unto you will be his desire — the desire of sin — that is, the evil inclination. It always strives and attempts to make you stumble." As a vegetarian, I might add in this context: Despite all the good will in the world, we are endowed with teeth, molars, which we share with the carnivorous animals. There is something within us which is opposed to that ethical ideal.

But there is another contradiction, and Rabbi Kook refers to it in his comments on a somewhat strange legend, the legend used by our Sages to interpret one detail in the story of creation. God commanded the earth to bring forth (Gen. 1:11) "any fruit tree yielding fruit;" but the earth did not do that, and brought forth (v. 12) only "the tree yielding fruit." The Talmudic legend emphasized the difference between these two expressions, "any fruit tree yielding fruit" and "any tree yielding fruit." It is as if the earth did not obey the command of God. Rabbi Kook was asked about this by one of his correspondents, and in his letter he wrote that the difference between the tree and its fruit is a symbol of the tragic relation between the aim and the means. Sometimes you have to reach an extremely sacred end, and you have no other means except means which include evil. Here we have the tragedy of a man, who is unable, or unprepared, to accept the pacifist advice of Rabbi Tomrat. He wishes to change reality, but he discovers the fact that there are trees which yield fruit, but are not themselves fruit trees.

There are also ends which are not always holy and right. There are rules of the game, which I must always keep. But if I am to guard my independence, I must sometimes enter this game, and make use of that very thing I am struggling against: evil itself.

But there is also another tragedy in this area of moral perplexities, and one might call it the tragedy of the pairing of faces. This is to be found wherever the moral ideals themselves are inconsistent with each other, and I cannot realize all of them. This a dialectical tragedy, impressively depicted by Rabbi Kook by using the symbols of Lurianic Kabbalah and asserting that the emanations (*sefirot*) themselves contradict each other. There are contradictions between the various ideals, and one must find a way, which is often a very tortuous way, of arriving at a synthesis between these ideals. This synthesis is the "pairing of the faces."

Usually, we teach our children that they must be good, as if we knew clearly what it was to be good. But in practice, we are often perplexed by the relation between ends and means, ideals and actions. We are confused by the various flags we wave, and these are not only symbols for problems of security and the economy, but also stand for moral ideals. We do not possess one single moral ideal. Very often, our different moral ideals bring about a clash, and when we follow one of these ideals but not the other, we automatically do evil. The whole secret is contained in the proper pairing of the various sides. This is the secret of the sexual symbolism of the Kabbalah in its practical application to the area of morals, as Rabbi Kook sees it. We must arrive at a proper pairing and union; we must bring about a synthesis of ideals which often appear before us as thesis and antithesis.

This reality, in which man finds himself drawn in different directions by good and evil is thus a dramatic reality, the reality of war and struggle. It is not merely a matter of doing good, but also of searching for the good, of detecting concrete good in given historical situations. It is a good which includes shells, but also sparks.

We remember, for example, the words of Rabbi Tomrat on slavery and the ideology which created slavery. As against it, Rabbi

Kook presents a sober view, maintaining that slavery cannot be abolished if there are not sufficient conditions for its abolition. There is a necessity inherent in the human condition that some people should be slaves and — if not legally slaves, slaves by selling their labor for the sake of their subsistence. This is to say that reality itself shows us that the legal abolition of slavery did not do away with the fact of slavery, since the state of the proletariat is, in fact, a state of slavery. "And the liberation was no gain at all in the generality of the human race, except inasmuch as the need for slave-labor in general has decreased."

We may, of course, uphold the very beautiful ideal of pacifism, utopianism and the like, after the fashion of Rabbi Tomrat. But Rabbi Kook maintains that this is not what we need now. What we need is moral illuminations. We have to look after the life of the workers, both from the material and the moral points of view. We are in a given situation — let us call it capitalist society. I may not be happy with this state of affairs, but I cannot change it. The rich man's heart is sealed off, and he ridicules justice and morality. As Rabbi Kook has it: "It is easier for him to have no light and air in the tunnels of the mines, thus shortening the lives of hundreds of thousands of people, so long as he does not have to spend hundreds of thousands of pounds" in order to improve the conditions in the mine. If sometimes there is a landslide in the mine and some of his laborers are buried alive, the employer could not care less, since he is likely to find other laborers. This is our reality.

We have to fight against this reality, but it is a reality we cannot repair. It is possible — and I myself have no doubt about it —that there is salvation at the end of the tunnel. But our struggle must be a historical struggle, which takes reality into account. It is a struggle in which, unfortunately, good and evil are intermixed. This is the source of the basic intuition of the shells and the sparks.

IX.

Between Imagination and Joy

In the previous chapters, we discussed the Kabbalistic approach to our problem and depicted some of its characteristics. By and large, we saw how the Kabbalah stresses the reality of evil and of the struggle between the two forces, and how it assumes not only the existence of such a struggle within man himself, in the anthropological sense, but also outside him, between the two forces of good and evil, holiness and the Other Side, the *sitra ahara*. But there are also in the Kabbalah other directions and other tendencies. For the Kabbalah includes, beside legendary, pictorial, and almost mythical elements, some abstract philosophical delineations.

It is one of these philosophical tendencies which I wish to review here now. This philosophical — one might almost say, idealistic — tendency can be found in different periods and in the writings of different thinkers, but in order to make it more concrete, I will make use once more of the work of Rabbi Abraham Isaac Kook, to which we have already referred a few times. His work draws largely on the sources of the Kabbalah and Hasidism, although it is often presented in a modern garb. The present chapter will therefore bring us closer to the manner in which the Hasidic movement interpreted the Kabbalah, and to the implications of such an interpretation to the problem of good and evil.

As we have already noted in a previous chapter, Rabbi Kook depicts, in one of his writings, evil as something real, something which exists, whose being cannot be denied or ignored by us. For, in

82

its essence, there is a *desire* for evil, something like what Freud called Thanatos, a desire for evil, for destruction, which exists throughout the world.

Rabbi Kook depicts evil as a tree. But, like all trees in the imagery of the Kabbalah, it is a tree which stands upside-down, with its roots pointing up and its trunk and top downward. For we must look at reality "the other way round." Thus we have a tree with its roots in heaven and its trunk and branches down below.

This tree is evil. Like every tree, it has its roots and its trunk. The distinction between roots and trunk also applies to it. But what we can see of it is only the trunk, since the roots are hidden from us. Here we have the paradox, which is that evil is indeed evil, but its roots are good. Its roots are in the region of the good. Thus, the reality which we face, and which appears to be evil, is indeed evil — but it is evil only because of the way we conceive of it. We conceive of evil, since we can see only the trunk and the branches of the tree. But in its roots, this tree is good, drawing its nourishment from the good. It is we alone who cannot understand this, since the roots are covered and are apparently under the earth. But one should remember that in the language of Kabbalistic symbolism, under the earth means in heaven, or above the heavens, which is the area we cannot observe.

In the final count, what we have here is an idealistic approach, which depicts reality as an illusion. But one should also remember that this is a partial illusion — an illusion as to the trunk, but not as to the roots. For there is a certain reality which remains hidden from us. The things which we perceive are not real or, to use a philosophical term, they are not "the thing in itself." The thing in itself is not perceived by us.

It is true that we do perceive evil, and this is one more of our perceptions of reality. But the truth is that we could say that reality has camouflaged itself. What we have before us is a screen or a veil, and reality as it appears to us is not true reality.

We could, if we wished, use philosophical categories — Kantian or other — to describe these two strata of reality. Rabbi Kook uses a term which is very widespread in Hasidic thought and has its roots in Medieval Jewish thought — "imagination." Thus we conceive of reality by means of the imagination, but imagination appears here in a different sense from the usual one. It is not as though evil were imaginary, but only that by means of our instruments of perception, by means of our epistemological apparatus, we conceive of reality in a certain way. This apparatus is called imagination. It is, of course, extremely difficult to transcend this imagination, and Rabbi Kook says explicitly that coming out of the imagination is like escaping from prison — "from the career of reality." Just as, if you are in prison, you cannot, as a prisoner, set yourself free, so is it impossible for us to set ourselves free from that reality. But we must also know that this is not the real world, and that there is the possibility that we might come out of that prison, that imaginary cell.

This approach has its roots in the Hasidic position on the problem of good and evil. We also find its main outlines in the writings of one of the most profound Jewish thinkers of modern times, Rabbi Moshe Hayim Luzzato. In his book *Da'at Tevunot*, Luzzato depicts the human predicament in a manner which could be illustrated by the model of the theater which we have used more than once in the earlier chapters.

We are witnessing, indeed, a drama which unfolds before our eyes. It is something of a play, but a play which, in the last resort, was created, as it were, in order to deceive us. We are the dupes of this play, since this play is not the real thing which is taking place. This can be discerned in the fact that, when we speak or think of reality, we are liable to err. We could, for example, assume that there is, in this reality, no creator, no reward and no punishment. Luzzato himself stresses two errors which are of special relevance to our issue. One of them is dualism, in the light of which reality is conceived by us as a struggle between two forces, the force of good and the force of evil. The other, which will assume greater importance as we proceed with these talks, is the destiny of the Jewish people. The history and the destiny of the Jewish people seem to prove the opposite of what they are out to demonstrate. The tragic history of the Jewish people appears to be a proof that the

Torah cannot be right. This was precisely the argument of Christianity, which used the Jewish people as proof of its own position, and the destiny of the exiled Jewish people as a demonstration that Jesus is the Messiah. The Jews, because they refused to accept him, have been scattered and humiliated through all corners of the inhabited world.

It is a fact that history, as well as the whole of reality, appears to point to the existence of two forces. But this is a mere drama, expressing a situation which has been created only in a drama. One might say that it has been created in order to produce the opposite effect — to put us through the great trial of faith. This trial is meant to test us and see whether we can stand the test and realize the great principle of Judaism, the principle of the unity of God. This, despite the fact that in the world there appear to be two sides, and evil exists beside good. The problem is whether we can still hold on to our faith.

Both Luzzato and later thinkers stress this very idea — which appears to me to have reached its most intense expression in the writings of Rabbi Kook — the idea that, in fact, the reality which is rooted in evil is not the reality which we perceive. We can thus arrive at a formulation which would sound strange on first hearing, the fascinating dictum of the great teacher of philosophy in the Hebrew University of Jerusalem, Samuel Hugo Bergmann: death is merely a mistake. This is a paradoxical statement, which maintains that we judge everything by means of the things we conceive, that is, by means of human consciousness and through the instruments of human perception. But, since these instruments do not describe reality, since they are mere human instruments of perception, death does not exist in reality. If, at any stage, we reach an overall and true understanding of reality, we will then understand that death is not and that evil is not.

If we were to remain at this stage, we would be left within certain streams of Hasidic or Kabbalistic thought. But Rabbi Kook has an additional principle, which is of interest and importance, and of special relevance to our age. I refer to his idea that the process of our awakening from error, as it were, is a process which has historical implications.

Let us take a very simple example. There is a *motif* which can be found frequently in Hasidic literature. It is a comment on the verse in Psalms 126:1, which we all remember from the Grace after Meals on the Sabbath: "When the Lord turned again the captivity of Zion, we were like them that dream."

The dominant feeling here is that we are, in fact, in the midst of a dream, which is different from the dreams we have at night. For what we have here is a dream in installments — a dream which we know we will continue to dream once more tomorrow, when we have awakened from the interval of the dream, which is sleep and its dreams. According to this perception, we are, indeed, in the midst of a dream, a dream which has its own rules, but this does not make it cease to be a dream. In Hasidic thought, one of the most outstanding ideas is that our exile is nothing but a dream, from which we are to awaken. This idea also appears as an allegory in the writings of the founders of Zionism, who speak of the predicament of the Jewish people as of a dream from which one should awaken.

But the situation here is far more complex. This is no mere allegory. It is a claim that reality is not what we conceive it to be, and that, although it may appear to us in a very vivid manner, it is not as real as it seems. This is just as a dream I am having is not real, although it can bring on me a state of immense oppression and unbearable suffering. It still remains a dream. Now, salvation is the awakening from this dream. It is like waking up. We can open our eyes, and when we look back on what has happened, we will realize that everything which has taken place is nothing but a dream, and that reality is very different. This approach, which I have depicted here in its extreme form, would exemplify the sort of thinking with we are concerned.

But this is not exactly the thought of Rabbi Kook, who drew on this approach but developed a position which was somewhat different from it. This he did because he believed in an evolution which takes place within the historical process. In his opinion, our awakening from the dream takes place in history, and is to be discerned in the fact that evil is slowly disappearing and being conquered, while good has enlarged its domain. Our awakening will therefore find its expression in the improvement and perfection of the world, in the fact that society and the world will become better every day, and that the good will win in the world.

In simple terms, Rabbi Kook believed in progress and development. He believed in the idea of progress — which implies that time will do its work or, in the words of the popular saying which has much wisdom in it: time will do what reason will not. If so, time — in the very fact that it goes on — is a positive factor, which is to lead the world to progress and development.

Such an observation of the world is, no doubt, optimism, and it relies not only on an analysis of history itself, but also on the assumption that the processes of history correspond to processes which occur in the universe. Rabbi Kook was familiar with the theory of evolution and accepted it in principle, although his reasons were very different from those of Darwin. One can also detect a certain closeness to Bergson in his conception of reality as a development toward the good and toward perfection. Our world, in the view of Rabbi Kook, is not a perfect world, but it has in it the principle of perfectibility. This perfectibility leads the universe into development, brings life to a realization, and propels society in the direction of a good development, which is the development of history.

Thus, the meaning of salvation is progress and the victory of good, and we can depict it as an ascending line. It is true — and this is important — that there are sometimes *loops* in this line. We are also faced with descents and even with sharp falls. But these are mere *loops*, while the positive progress towards good continues. Assume, for example, that we are now in France, in the period of the reign of terror which followed the French Revolution. What we would be witnessing is destruction, the revocation, if not the absolute reversal, of all the ideas which prompted the Revolution. But this would only be a *loop*, or a fall — just as the episode of the Golden Calf, following on the giving of the Law at Mount Sinai, was a fall, which is sometimes inevitable.

87

Thus, if we look back on it today, we find out that despite all the terror and suffering, there was real progress achieved, and the French Revolution was part of this progress. Similarly, it is possible that other events which we are witnessing today in relation to other revolutions, surrounded by horrors like Gulags and concentration camps — that these, too, realize part of a process which, in the long run, will be revealed as good. Falls do occur, and there are traps on the way of every process of salvation — but we must put our full faith in the victory of good or in the positive direction of historical development. This is a necessity.

Rabbi David Ha-Cohen, the Nazirite, a pupil of Rabbi Kook, illustrated this with the example of joined vessels. Let us imagine that we have two vessels which are linked in the shape of the letter U. At the one end, water is poured into this U-shaped vessel from a large reservoir of water, and it rises to the same level on the other side. This rise may be hard, but it is necessary. The reservoir, a reservoir of light to which we are linked, is perfection, or God. The world draws, in its origin, from God, and therefore its development is to the good. Victory should be conceived as a fact, despite all the retreats and all the lapses. A similar process takes place in human history. Good must prevail, and it will prevail, in spite of all lapses, and although we always live in the feeling that we are in the throes of one of these falls and crises, and see no way out.

One can see in these words a faith in progress and an expression of Kabbalistic ideas applied to, and represented in, history. It is a fact that Kabbalistic symbolism regarding the battle between good and evil was, on the one hand, inspired by history, and, on the other hand, it also interpreted history and made it possible for Kabbalists and other thinkers to interpret history. This is especially true of Lurianic Kabbalah, which maintains that we can understand the events of our history by means of that symbolism of the battle against evil and the "perfecting" of the world — a process in which we are partners.

Hasidic thought was essentially optimistic, and this is even more true of the more popular aspects of Hasidic thought. In this context, it may be appropriate to cite here the story of the man who asked the Maggid of Mezritch, "Why is it that there are righteous people who suffer and wicked people who prosper?" The Maggid of Mezritch sent this man to Rabbi Zusia of Annipoli to pose the same question to him. Rabbi Zusia was one of the greatest and best-known figures among the Maggid's disciples. This man was sure that he would supply him with an answer, and he came and asked him his question. Rabbi Zusia replied: "I wonder why the Maggid told you to ask me this question. You should have asked someone who has suffered something evil, God forbid. As to me, this is irrelevant, since I have never suffered anything evil."

This story of Rabbi Zusia represents Hasidism in it popular form, as it is conceived by the ordinary people. This is not Hasidism at its profoundest. As we have already seen in our previous talks, one cannot ignore the fact that Hasidism, too, had its own Job in the person of Rabbi Nahman of Breslau. This was a thinker who raised Hasidism to new summits in his thinking about good and evil. He pointed out the need to reveal another dimension of good and evil, the existentialist dimension. We will discuss him in one of the following chapters.

X.

The Halachic Approach

Our relation to the Biblical position has been indirect: we have examined this position by means of various ways of approach which have been developed by various Jewish thinkers. But there can be no doubt that there are in the Bible two outstanding *motifs* related to the issue of good and evil, two *motifs* which were already utilized and developed by Rabbi Moses ben Nahman, known as *Ramban* or Nahmanides. One of them is, of course, the *motif* of reward and punishment, which is understood by Nahmanides from a Kabbalistic and mystical angle. In his opinion, the reason for our way of looking at the world, including the good and evil contained in it, is that we do not take into account two other dimensions of the world. Nahmanides means the idea of the survival of the soul, which implies that life does not end with death, and the idea of reincarnation. In his opinion, this was Elihu's message, contained in his answer to Job; an answer which asserted that if we are to understand the life of man, we must take previous lives into account, and only the secret of reincarnation — a secret which is frequently found in the Zohar, and especially in the comment on the section *Mishpatim* (Exodus 21-24) — can explain to us properly what happens in the world.

But this is only half the truth, one side of the coin. There is another *motif*, related to the doctrine of temptation. Evil constitutes some kind of test or temptation. Nahmanides depicts this idea of temptation in his commentary on Exodus 20:7 — a

90

comment which has been often quoted and exercised a conscious or subconscious influence on numerous thinkers — where he says that there is no creature which is not tempted by God. The rich man is tested to see if he will open his hand to the poor, and the poor man, to see if he can take his suffering without complaining. The whole world is, by and large, some sort of temptation.

To some extent, this was expressed in the Middle Ages through the model of the theater. In the last resort, all the world is a stage and each of us an actor. The best acting does not depend on the text of the play, but on the way in which each of us performs his role. Let us take as an example two actors, one playing a slave and the other playing a king. Does it matter at all which role each actor plays, when all we are concerned with is the quality of their act? The real hero is not the role, but the good actor.

Thus, we are all actors in the same play, and the protagonist may well be exactly the poor man, the sufferer, who, in his very existence, constitutes the greatest challenge in the world. It is his reactions which are awaited by God. There is a democratic flavor to this approach of Nahmanides, which tells us that each of us is the protagonist. Each of us, each single person, has a role, and it is up to him to know how to perform this role and make the best of his part. Thus, we should not judge what befalls us in the categories of reward and punishment but in different categories, the categories of trial and temptation. We have been given the script of a play and have been put in it, and we have been given a chance — which may not be the chance given to the king — but it is up to us to know what to do with this script.

Nahmanides' angle of observation can serve as the introduction to the world of thought of another thinker, one of our contemporaries, who now lives in Boston, Rabbi Joseph Dov Soloveichik, who is perhaps the most outstanding existentialist Jewish thinker of our day.

Rabbi Soloveichik deals with the problems of good and evil in the first part of his well-known essay, *The Voice of my Beloved is Knocking*, an essay which also deals, among other things, with the issues of Zionism and of Jewish existence today.

91

His starting-point is the Talmudic comment (B. *Berakhot* 7a) on the great vision in Exodus 33:13, where Moses asks to see God's glory and to know His way, and says: "Show me now Your way, that I may know You."

What was Moses actually asking here? The philosopher would doubtless say that he wanted to know the secrets of creation, or the attributes of God. Maimonides said something additional: he wanted to know the way God conducts His world. On this point, his position is very similar to that of our Talmudic passage. The Talmud interprets this verse in the simplest possible way: "He said before Him: 'Master of the universe, why is it that there are a righteous man who prospers, and a righteous man who suffers, and a wicked man who prospers, and a wicked man who suffers?'" This is Moses' question, as the Talmud interprets it. Thus, in the Talmudic view, the highest point of this vision is the quest for an answer to our central question, the question of good and evil. The Talmud continues: "And Rabbi Meir says: 'It was not given unto him'" — that is, God gave him no answer. For the answer, after all, is, "...And I will pardon whom I will pardon, and show mercy to whom I show mercy" (*ibid.* 16). In other words: you cannot have the answer. This Talmudic passage is also the point of departure of Rabbi Soloveichik's discussion.

But Rabbi Soloveichik takes us further, and shows that this was also the question of Habakkuk, who was defending the cause of justice when he saw (1:13) "the wicked devouring the man that is more righteous than he," as well as the question of Jeremiah, of David in the Book of Psalms, of Ecclesiastes, and, of course, of Job. Job is the central figure in Rabbi Soloveichik's essay.

What is, perhaps, the one clear and common point emerging from all our discussions so far is that Judaism is perplexed by evil and struggles against it, but it is not prepared to deny it. It is not prepared to live in the illusion that evil does not exist. Evil is a given fact, and an admission of this state of affairs brings us to the consideration of two possible positions or methods.

One of them is the position of fate, and the other, that of destiny or mission. The implications should be immediately clear to us. On the one hand, we have a situation in which you find yourself, and the explanation should refer to a previous cause. On the other hand, you have a mission which should be explained in reference to an aim or an end. The truth is that this essay contains more than these ideas. But we must first understand these two options facing us.

I therefore invite the reader to accompany me on a voyage of exploration of Rabbi Soloveichik's text. The problem which arises from it is, what is this fated existence? It is a fact that you are alive, whether you will or not. The fated ego accepts this as a fact, but the fated ego is an object. This reminds us of the image we have used in one of our previous talks, that of a puppet in a puppet theater, which is at the mercy of superior forces. The fated ego finds himself, in the terms of Rabbi Soloveichik, in a line of sealed dynamics, all oriented outward.

Man, then, is an object, and an object in fetters. This is one side of it. But this very same fated ego, thrown into this world, is nevertheless a philosopher. The interesting point is exactly this: he asks questions concerning good and evil. He has intellectual curiosity which strives to understand the world and what takes place in it. This is when he creates philosophy. This creation passes through a number of stages. The first stage (and here we feel how Rabbi Soloveichik offers us something like a philosophical interpretation of the Book of Job, since this stage is what we witness in the first few chapters of that Book) is the stage of silence. It is common to Job and every person who really knows what suffering is: the first, stunning shock.

The second stage is that of intellectual curiosity. Now we wish to understand the situation and digest it. We ask why. This is the stage at which philosophy enters. But what does philosophy actually do at this stage? What we have now is criticism of all that we read in our first chapters. What did philosophy accomplish by its doctrine of privation? It accomplished nothing except for the blurring of evil. It merely erased and blurred it, not wishing to hear of it.

It is at the third stage that philosophy develops a realistic approach to the predicament of man and his place in reality. Rabbi

Soloveichik's own words are that Judaism "understood that evil cannot be blurred and covered up." It understood that, when we speak of the best of all possible worlds, we enter into cooperation with evil. And he adds: "For any attempt to minimize the importance of contrast and division in the universe will bring man neither to his peace of mind nor to a grasp of any mystery of existence."

In other words, philosophy presented us with a fine piece of speculation, with an extremely interesting doctrine of evil, but it has not slaked our existential thirst. It *may* have offered — the emphasis here is on the word "may" — an intellectual solution. This can be seen already in Greek thought, which spoke of evil as privation and construed exquisite intellectual structures, but did not grasp the existential secret of evil. This secret remained, and remained concealed. Evil, Rabbi Soloveichik continues, is a fact which cannot be denied. There is evil, there is suffering, and there are torments of hell in this world. This is a fact which cannot be erased. Anyone who wishes to deceive himself by turning his thoughts away from the rift in the nature of being by means of a romanticization of human life, is a fool who sees hallucinations. Philosophy attempted to overcome the monster of evil by means of its analytical and speculative tools, through philosophical analysis or philosophical terminology or semantics. But it has not succeeded.

It cannot succeed, and it cannot give man a speculative answer which will put his mind at peace. This is why, as Judaism asserts, it would be in vain to look for a solution within speculative thought. We must look for it elsewhere.

This is a reaction against the attempt to sweep evil under the carpet. In this context, Rabbi Soloveichik has another observation to make. In our former chapters, we have examined the position which maintains that evil is only the result of our limited scope of vision; for, if we were able to see the whole picture, we would have seen only the good. This appears to be the interpretation of the verse (Gen. 1:31) "And God saw every thing that he had made, and, behold, it was very good." That is, in *everything* there is good for those who have eyes to see. Rabbi Soloveichik does not deny this, but he adds one detail, which he explains by means of an image. Let us look, he says, at a tapestry which contains an exquisitely beautiful picture. Unfortunately for us, we can see it only from the other side — not the side of the beautiful picture itself, but the side where the threads are tied together. Thus we are unable to see the beauty of the tapestry.

Indeed, says Rabbi Soloveichik, to our great misfortune, we can see the world only from its side. This is an existential interpretation of the concept of "the Other Side," the *sitra ahara*. What is the *sitra ahara*? We see the exquisite embroidery, but we see it only from the *sitra ahara*, from the other side. Thus, it would be in vain to look for a significance which does not exist. It exists for God, but we — Rabbi Soloveichik continues — are unable to grasp the overall texture of being, in which alone one can detect the plan and essence of God's creation. The answer is true and fine, but for us it is meaningless, since we see only the rift, the parts, the other side of this exquisite piece of tapestry, and are unable to understand it.

It follows that the view of evil from the angle of fated man must be closed to us. All that we have so far discussed, from the point of view of speculative philosophy, has led us to a dead end. This was because we have ignored another dimension of ourselves, which is different from that of the fated ego. There must also be a dimension of the ego of mission and destiny, from the vantage point of which one can see reality in a different fashion.

What is this ego? The first ego was an ego living despite itself. The ego of destiny has another motto. Imitating, with a slight change, a famous Talmudic maxim, his motto is: "Against your will you are born and against your will you die — but of your own free will you live." Man, says Rabbi Soloveichik, is born as an object and dies as an object — but he has the power of living as a subject, as a creator and innovator.

These two terms, object and subject, are Rabbi Soloveichik's rendering of a famous pair of concepts in the Talmud: *heftza* — a thing or instrument, and *gavra* — a man. These, according to him, are simply the Aramaic, Talmudic terms for object and subject.

There are men who live like objects — the fated man, who lives according to his fate. But man can also live as *gavra*, as a subject, as someone who puts his own individual seal on his own life, someone who transcends his automatic actions into the sphere of creative activity.

These are, in fact two things — on the one hand, creative activity, and on the other hand, the individual seal. We are not dealing here with collective activity alone, but each single individual is estimated in his own right and has a significance in his own right. What, then is the purpose of man? His purpose is to turn fate into destiny, and to turn himself from being influenced into being influential; from existing despite himself, an existence in perplexity and muteness, in that dumb silence which man has not been able to transcend, into someone who realizes a life full of will, elevation and initiative.

What would be the approach to the problem of evil of the man who lives the life of mission and destiny? Evil will be, for him, no mere speculative problem. His starting point is moral and *halachic*, devoid of any speculative metaphysical strain. If I understand Rabbi Soloveichik properly, we cannot understand and penetrate the mystery of evil. Even Moses could not do this. We are thrown into a world which contains evil. The question is, what am I to do in this given situation — and this is a question of *halachah*, of morality, not a theological question.

The suffering man of destiny can only say: "There is evil. I do not deny it and I do not attempt to cover it up with idle speculations." Covering up, in Rabbi Soloveichik's terms, is probably the exact counterpart of the term "theodicy." His approach is: "I am interested in evil from the *halachic* point of view, as a man who wants to know which action he is to take. I ask a simple question: what will the sufferer do in order to live with his suffering? The result of my enquiry should be how to live with evil. I am looking for an answer to the problem, how to live in a world of suffering, how to live while I am suffering."

The answer, therefore, is a *halachic* answer. Suffering, says Rabbi Soloveichik, comes in order to purify man, to elevate his spirit, and to sanctify him. In other words, it comes as part of the calculus of reward and punishment. I do not know this calculus and cannot understand it. But suffering offers me some kind of opportunity. This brings us to the paradoxical idea which is expressed by what is, perhaps, the most powerful sentence in this essay: "The *halachah* teaches us that it is a major sin for a man who suffers to let his pains remain meaningless and to be left without any aim or significance."

In a paradoxical manner, we have arrived here at an existential interpretation of the problem of temptation, of the sort we have already seen in the words of Rabbi Moses ben Nahman, Nahmanides, for, as we saw, Nahmanides maintains that each man — the rich man as well as the poor man — is being tested. The master and the slave are being tried. The question is, what is this trial or temptation? What am I to do with the suffering which has befallen me? Now, Nahmanides says in his commentary: "'It is even the time of Jacob's trouble, but he shall be saved out of it' (Jer. 30:7): Out of his trouble itself will he be redeemed for ever." He will achieve an unparalleled strengthening and elevation in a world devoid of suffering. These words do not give us an interpretation of suffering or a covering up for suffering. Their position is unambiguous: there is suffering, and I have to learn a lesson from it. In a paradoxical manner, it should help me construct my world. This fact could be described by saying that a thesis emerges from an anti-thesis.

Rabbi Soloveichik, in his usual manner, gives this idea a *halachic* expression. There are, he says, two types of commandments concerning repentance. There is the commandment that man must "make" his repentance, and this commandment is included by Maimonides in his *halachot* concerning repentance. But there is also the duty of a different kind of repentance, the repentance at a time of tribulation. The Bible itself (Num. 10:9) says: "And if you go to war in your land ... you shall be remembered before the Lord your God." Thus war and suffering should make us take count of our lives, not because we claim that the suffering has come because of some act of ours, but for a different reason — because we have to look at life from a different point of view. This is no longer part of the *halachot* concerning repentance, but of the *halachot* concerning fasts — of the laws regarding the tribulations of the community and the individual, and of a completely different vision of the good.

If this is so, Rabbi Soloveichik continues, then "woe unto the sufferer, if his soul has not been warmed by the fire of suffering." In the final count, this is a tragedy in which the same fire which is burning a man also warms him. Woe unto the man who has wasted his suffering. Job stood, in the long run, the test of two temptations. He stood the test of wealth, and now he had to stand the test of poverty. It would be interesting to look at the ending of his story and ask: at what point was Job redeemed? Job was saved when he began to pray for his companions. At that point (Job 42:10), "the Lord turned the captivity of Job," as he was praying for his companions. This is the true answer to the sufferings of Job. Here we can see that Job has learned from suffering, has understood the sufferer, and has come to regard himself as part of the human community. He has learned to see and hear the sufferings of others as well. He prayed for the others, and God saved him too.

XI.

In the Wake of the Holocaust

The previous chapters dealt with philosophical texts on the one hand, and with pictorial images by means of which the Kabbalah expressed its approach to the problem of good and evil. But it appears that now we have come to the point at which we should change our direction and deal with very painful existential and historical problems, with open wounds which exist in each of us, and which show that the problem of good and evil is no mere academic issue, nor is it only an individual issue, but a problem which touches the depths of our existence.

I refer to the influence of the Holocaust on Jewish thought and to its repercussions; to the various reactions of Jewish thinkers to it insofar as it is a problem of good and evil. We opened this work with a picture from the ancient world. We then moved on to Medieval philosophy. We examined the approach of more recent thinkers, taken from the world of Hasidism. Now we have reached what could be called a moment of truth for philosophy. We now have to examine the way in which it relates to this problem and reacts to it.

There are, of course, the well-known classical reactions, some of which were documented while the Holocaust was still in its midst. But as a first step, let me stress the fact that what we are discussing here is something which certain thinkers have called a radical evil. I do not know how to explain or interpret such a term, and I shall therefore attempt to transmit to you the experience out of which, as I see it, such a term has grown.

Let us examine three possible types of murderers. First, there is the opportunist. I can think of no stronger word which would really suit the character of the Polish peasant who handed over a Jew to the Germans because he coveted his boots. The other figure is that of the sadist, the man who enjoys causing suffering to others. Both are figures which also exist in our normal world. In addition to them, a new image grew in the Holocaust, and I shall call it — with a few sets of quotation marks — the "idealist." I refer to the man who did evil for its own sake, and to a certain extent was not even aware of doing evil. Problems and reactions concerning this figure arose during the Eichmann Trial in Jerusalem. It appears, though, that this figure embodies radical evil.

Bearing such distinctions in mind, let us now turn to an examination of the reactions of Jewish thinkers to the Holocaust. We will soon see that thought on this issue is distinctly divided into two camps, and I regard this as the most fundamental controversy which has arisen since the Holocaust. On the one hand, we have people who believe that they have an explanation to offer to these events. I shall mention two examples of people who believe that they can offer an explanation of what took place: Hannah Arendt and Bruno Bettelheim. Their explanations are in categories which are taken from other fields; psychology and sociology.

On the other hand, there are other thinkers — and I have in mind Elie Wiesel, Emil Fackenheim and others — who think that what we are faced with here is an evil which is fundamentally different and is not open to any rational explanation whatsoever. The Holocaust was, for them, a revelation of evil, almost a mystical revelation, one of cosmic dimensions which is unparalleled, in which we have an expression of a kind of wickedness which is not open to any interpretation, be it psychological or sociological. Here, I believe, we have the root of the controversy.

Such thinkers treat the Holocaust as a question which can have no answer. Some of them regard it as an event of cosmic dimensions, something like an antithesis to the giving of the Law on Mount Sinai; as a phenomenon from which we have to learn, and in the light of which our whole life must change, for, in this

100

phenomenon, we have been faced by an evil which is unlike any other evil, not in its intensity, but in its very essence.

In the light of such thinking, the difference between the Holocaust and Hiroshima is not quantitative. Even if twenty more bombs like the Hiroshima bomb had been dropped, we would still have nothing which resembles the Holocaust in its essence. People have been massacred in other wars. In Cambodia and Indonesia, people have been massacred by the millions for their political affiliations. There have already been events in human history which could be defined as genocide. But none of them is identical with the Holocaust.

The principle thesis of such thought — and this, I believe, is its greatest contribution to the development of the doctrine of evil in our age — is the thesis which maintains that we are faced here with an evil which is different in its nature and essence. The persecution of people for political reasons is, of course, an evil which we must fight. Mass murder is an unparalleled crime, a crime against humanity. But the Holocaust was something essentially different. The intention and the activity involved in the murder of a Jewish child, the form in which it was perpetrated, the aim for which it was done, and the background of its execution — all these are totally different in every sense from all the other massacres and intended massacres in history.

Let us stop here to examine some immediate reactions to the Holocaust. Doubtless, one can find among religious thinkers some reactions which draw on the classical and popular position that one can regard evil as a punishment. What is, perhaps, the most shocking document of this sort is a book, published in Budapest, the capital of Hungary, in Hanukkah 5704, December 1943. It is called *The Joyful Mother of Children*, and it reached us in this country by a tortuous way just before the 1967 war. It was by then a rare book, and it was reprinted by people who are close to the approach expressed in it and who find in this book a position with which they can identify.

The book was written by Rabbi Issachar Solomon Teichtel, who was, until the outbreak of the Second World War, close to the extreme Orthodox position of Natorei Karta. He wrote it during the years of the War, under the Fascist Hungarian regime. Rabbi Teichtel had seen what he had seen and had changed his mind. The book is an act of repentance for his former repudiation of Zionism. For it was, he believed, the rejection of Zionism or a misapprehension of it which had brought him, the community he belonged to, and the entire Jewish people in Europe, to the great tragedy they were living through.

No doubt other opinions were also expressed then. Some of the Jews of Hungary continued in the way of the Rebbe of Satmar and others, claiming that one should put some of the blame at the gate of assimilationism and Zionism. But Rabbi Teichtel's book is clearly what can be described as a document of the authentic thought of a man who judges reality, condemns it, and changes his mind in the light of the events which he sees taking place in his generation.

Another example, which could serve as the diametrical opposite, is that of a Reform Jewish thinker, which aroused great echoes in the United States — the thought of Richard Rubenstein. Rubenstein, in his book, *After Auschwitz*, propounded the thesis that the Holocaust broke our link with the symbolic system of Judaism, and that there was now, in the last resort, no place for belief in a God of salvation.

These are two opposite positions. The first expresses the continued adherence to classical Jewish categories, while the second is the expression of rebellion, of coming out in condemnation of the classical categories, and the search for what Rubenstein himself described, in the strongest words, as Jewish neo-paganism, the return to a Jewish paganism or to a similar position, rather than that of classical Judaism, or what Rubenstein called the framework of the Aggadah (Jewish legend and exegesis).

Between these two extreme positions, one can point to other thinkers who attempted to express their reactions and to draw an entirely different lesson from those events. But at this point I would rather abandon this examination of the different positions, and attempt to examine once again with you a book which has been our constant companion in our previous discussions, the Book of Job.

The Book of Job, as we have seen, depicts the sufferings of the individual. But it is interesting that, from time to time, it is regarded by commentators as describing not the sufferings of the individual, but of the whole Jewish nation. Thus, it is not a mere allegory of the troubles of a single human being, but a symbol of the whole people of Israel. This idea is already found in the ancient Midrashic work, *Pesikta*, and it emerges again and again from what appears to be a long sleep. We find it in the views of Solomon Molcho, and then again in Martin Buber. Thus it emerges again and again, as if Job himself had already hinted at it.

But what is the great lesson of the Book of Job? One of its lessons is the suffering Job. His companions arrive and attempt to teach him that he is suffering because he is a sinner. But what we have in the book is something of a reversal of the classical position. For Eliphaz has maintained that Job should understand the fact of his suffering and realize that it is proof of his sin, whereas the great lesson of the book is that this position is wrong. God Himself tells Job's companions later that it is they who have sinned by believing that Job's sufferings had been brought about by sin. But is there anything which is more suitable to the historical situation of the Jewish people? The Jewish people is in trouble. It also has companions: Christianity, Islam, and other positions, neo-pagan and the rest, which come up to it and claim: you are suffering for your sins, and the proof of the injustice of your case is your suffering itself. The proof that you are not right is the fact that you are scattered to the four corners of the world. Since you have not accepted this or that truth, since you have not put your faith in the Savior, or in the Prophet, you must be humiliated, and your suffering will be a sign to all others. The cancelling of this fundamental equation is now seen as the core of the Book of Job, since this book teaches us that the classical Jewish position was by no means as simple-minded as people would wish to believe. It did not say that punishment is the result of sin. The most distinct example of this is the Book of Job, and this is why it has been included among the Scriptures. To regard the Holocaust in those categories of sin and punishment would be to repeat the error of Job's companions.

If you wish, we can say that we have now come close to an interesting and disturbing question. For one can understand the answer given by the Book of Job in different ways. One person can find it in the Hymn to Wisdom in Chapter 28, the search for a wisdom which may not be open to man or within his grasp. Another can seek it in the words of Elihu, the meaning of which has been disputed by the commentators. But at the same time, there is no doubt that the final point of this answer is to be found in the conclusion of the book, and is centered about two points. The first is that God reveals Himself to Job and says very strange things to him. He asks him some rhetorical questions: Do you know this or that? Do you understand the secrets of nature which are not revealed to man? You do not know the mystery of the universe. You do not even know the mystery of Leviathan; But what is the meaning of all this? One could say that the answer is of an agnostic nature, in the original sense of the word: you must realize that you are standing before a mystery which you cannot comprehend. But at the same time, it appears to me that there is more to it than that. God's answer to Job is, in fact, astonishment: I, who can distinguish between the most minute elements of the universe — could I be incapable of distinguishing between Job and my enemy? This is the whole answer. It simply means: know that these things have their hidden meaning, and that I am not your enemy. This answer is also expressed in the cry of faith after its desperation, in the possibility of continued faith even after Auschwitz, the possibility to go on believing even after our sufferings. The confrontation with God is, after all, not a confrontation with the absurd, but a confrontation with the mysterious. Those thinkers who draw this conclusion attempt, by means of it, to express their struggle to save the Holocaust from demythologization. This is to say, there is the tendency to draw these things into the daylight, to speak of them, so as to take them out of the mythical mist in which they have been enshrouded. But this type of thought wishes precisely to leave them in that mist and to stop treating the Holocaust in the categories we employ in all our other relations. It wishes to grasp it and to understand it in a different manner.

It is not — as Hannah Arendt said of Eichmann in her discussion of his trial — as if we were faced with a "bureaucrat of evil." What we have here is something demonic and Satanic which revealed itself to us.

But there is another point in the Book of Job which we should note. The book does not end with God's revelation, but with God "turning the captivity of Job." Job has new sons and daughters. When the reader is faced with this story, he cannot help remarking cynically: but the old sons did not, after all, return. This is, no doubt, not the solution we would have all expected — and even the believer in reincarnation would have expected: that Job would now have the same sons he had in the past.

Nevertheless, I believe that there is still something which we should learn from this picture of the sons born to Job, a principle related to our possible reaction to the problem of good and evil. The sense of these things raises for us a very hard problem: does the Holocaust mean that history has been abandoned, or is there still sense in my belief that, despite all, there is the possibility of the triumph of good in history and in a historical redemption? Do I continue to believe that history can be repaired and salvaged?

I believe that, at this point, we return to an idea which we have seen before in the doctrines of Rabbi Abraham Isaac Kook. We are faced with two fundamental positions. One of them could be described as a position of alienation. We are aliens and strangers in the world, which is an evil world. The other position maintains that, despite everything, history will reach salvation, and salvation is possible even after the Holocaust. From the individual's point of view, Job's new children are an absurdity. But from the point of view of the community, the revival of a nation is, indeed, possible. It is true that the Book of Job embodies the existential position of a man who is facing the mystery and does not know how to react to it, but he must go on believing even after he has discovered that it is a mystery. But there is more to the book than that. It also contains the claim that we cannot abandon history, that we cannot abandon the world. Thus we believe that God will turn the captivity of Job, and we detect in this turn of the captivity of Job the same symbol revealed to us "when the Lord turned again the captivity of Zion" and "we were like them that dream."

We have examined, in this chapter, a few positions. What emerges —and this could be our conclusion — is that Jewish thinkers found themselves torn between the absurdity of the Holocaust and its trauma. At the same time, they also attempted to think of the possibility of a new beginning of history and of the possibility or redemption, which finds its expression, not only within the individual, but also in human history.

XII.

Constructive Suffering

The problem of good and evil is one of those subjects which are by no means the sole property of academic philosophy, of the philosophy of the schools. It can be characterized, more accurately, as an existential issue. After all, it is tied up with the life of every human being, and it therefore constitutes a borderline area which embodies the close tie between life and thought. Of course, every philosophy is related to life, and the question is only how remote it is from life. As against issues discussed by ontology or by epistemology, which are regarded as remote from life, the problem of good and evil embodies something which is close to life, even to the life of each individual person. In this context, we would be justified in talking of a philosophy which is "engaged" — which reacts to the problem of the moment.

In the last generation, there have been two thinkers whose thought on the issue of good and evil has been outstanding and distinct — Martin Buber and Hillel Zeitlin. Martin Buber's name has been mentioned here more than once. His works on our issue exist in Hebrew in a book called *Images of Good and Evil — A Collection Concerning People*. These are lectures which began many years earlier, and which Buber wrote in their final form in the 1950's.

Buber's main concern in this book is to confront the Jewish attitude with that of Persia; Jewish monotheism against the dualism of ancient Persia and Gnosticism, as two divergent world pictures.

This is "engaged" philosophy, since Buber regarded the very existence of the Gnostic point of view as a grave danger — in fact, as one of the greatest dangers threatening the modern world. The danger is that Gnosticism regards what is within as if it were outside us. Let us elucidate this point by means of Buber's own words in another book, which was also written in the wake of the Holocaust — in fact, in the very midst of the period of the Holocaust, in 1941, and was first printed in installments in the daily newspaper *Davar*. The book is *Gog and Magog*, which Buber subtitles "a chronicle of days." It deals with the figure of the legendary King Gog of the land of Magog, whose wars, according to the prophecies of Ezekiel, are to precede the coming of the Messiah, as well as with the Talmudic tradition and Jewish mysticism.

Buber himself writes that the main point of the story is in the things said by the pupil to his master. I quote:

Rabbi, he said in a muted voice — and what is the business of this Gog? After all, his very existence outside us is because he is here within us. (He pointed a finger at his heart.) It is the darkness out of which he has been hewn. We must get him out of our sluggish and deceitful hearts. It is our betrayal of God which has fattened Gog until he has grown so mighty.

Buber's "message" is that Gog's origin is not outside us, but within the human heart. it is here, in the human heart, that the drama is enacted. It is here that we fatten and cherish and create the monster which is without. The book thus sets out to present us with the Jewish approach as against the Persian approach, and this is how it is construed.

We have mentioned Buber. But I wish to devote most of the present chapter to the second of these thinkers, Hillel Zeitlin. Just as Buber contrasts his view with the Persian view, so does Zeitlin confront the views of India and Greece. But before we examine the nature of this contrast, let us say a few words about the man and his book.

Hillel Zeitlin is almost unknown to the Israeli reader, although he was a wonderful man. His son, the poet Aaron Zeitlin, writes the following words in his biography of his father: "He resided in our world between 1871 and 1942, when, donning his *tallit* and *tefillin*, with the Book of Zohar in his hands, he sanctified the Name of God, having made the Benediction before Martyrdom."

Zeitlin wrote his book originally as a series of articles published, as early as 1899, in the Hebrew periodical *Ha'shiloah*, as "Good and Evil." The editor of *Ha'shiloah* at the time was Ahad Ha'am. Zeitlin dedicated his articles to his friend, Joseph Hayim Brenner. There was at the time a group of writers who regularly wrote for *Ha'shiloah*. They were people who searched for new ways. Apart from Zeitlin, who came from a Hasidic family but who had detached himself somewhat from his past, it included Uri Nissan Gnessin, Alman Yitzhak Anochi or Aaronson, and another young man, Shalom Sanderbaum, who is described by Aaron Zeitlin as a unique personality, a Stoic and a philosopher. This young man was a profound student of the problems of man, and later committed suicide. His suicide left a strong impression on his two friends, Brenner and Zeitlin, and made them search their ways. Each of them turned in a different direction. Brenner turned Sanderbaum into one of the heroes of his novel, *Around the Point*, in which he is referred to by the pseudonym Uriel Davidowski. Zeitlin discovered his way back to the old Hasidic melody, and remained part of his people — or, in his own phrase, "living among the population of Israel," until 1942, when he died for the sanctification of the Name of God.

The book we shall discuss belongs to an earlier period, but even there, we already discover the way in which Hillel Zeitlin sought to find a solution to the problem of good and evil. What Zeitlin offers us in this book, in a fascinating manner, is the history of this issue. In doing this, he confronts us with three approaches which are different from each other, not so much in the answers they supply as in the questions they raise. These are the positions of ancient Israel, Greece and India.

The Greek inquires about the suffering of man, with a special interest shown in the destiny of the hero. One might say that the Greeks raise the problem of man faced by the elements of nature, struggling against them, and failing and suffering as a result of this

109

struggle. The suffering of man, or of the hero, is the problem posed by ancient Greece. The Indian raises another problem. He, too, sets himself in front of the forces of nature and raises the question of evil in itself. Israel, in Zeitlin's opinion, raises the problem of justice and the sorrows of the righteous. This is not so much the problem of evil as it is the problem of justice. Be that as it may, Zeitlin's analysis stresses that, although the problem of evil has been raised in all civilizations, various nations have raised it in a different fashion and have given different answers to it.

We are faced, then, with three positions. In fact, the position of Judaism is confronted with two modern positions — that of Schopenhauer, who is the philosopher who translated into modern terms the ancient Indian position, and that of Nietzsche, who is regarded by Zeitlin as the man who translated into modern terms the ancient Greek position of the struggling hero. Beside these two positions, Zeitlin also mentions another modern one, with slight variations — the position of modern scientific positivism in its various versions. Against this background, Zeitlin investigates the position of Judaism, and his starting point is the question of whether the time has come to reassess our view of Judaism as a civilization with optimistic characteristics. Perhaps we have been mistaken, and we must reassess the familiar materials.

I should mention here that this was Schopenhauer's great accusation against Judaism. One might even say that Schopenhauer detested Judaism and fought against it, because he detected in it a will to live and to exist. It was against this will that he struggled.

Zeitlin, however, tells us that we should understand the position of Judaism in a different manner. We should be aware of the fact that there are within Judaism pessimistic strains as well, and that Judaism is fully aware of the existence of evil in the world, and the problem raised by it. Zeitlin pointed, in this connection, to the mystical tradition of the Kabbalah, as well as to the Biblical tradition itself, which contains not only the sentiment of goodness, but also a book like *Ecclesiastes*. Moreover, Judaism raises an additional problem. In its view, the man who suffers, suffers twice — once, because he is suffering, but over and above that, also because his suffering has no sense. If man could only find meaning in his suffering, his whole feeling would have changed. Here, a number of alternatives offer themselves in the attempt to find meaning to suffering, and this is where man's perplexity begins. At this point, Zeitlin enters into a dialogue with Nietzsche as well as with Schopenhauer, as Rabbi Kook also did in his philosophical diaries, *Oroth ha-Kodesh.*

In this context, Zeitlin presents two reactions to the same reality — the position of Buddha and that of the Baal Shem Tov. Zeitlin maintains that though ancient India saw reality as *non-being* and reacted to this *non-being*, the Jew — the Baal Shem Tov — also saw in it *non-being*, but in it was concealed, in his view, a divine entity. Hence the difference, which implies for the Jew that despite everything, despite the feeling of suffering, we have attained some significance, and we can proceed to build on the basis of this significance. Suffering has thus turned into something which helps man build himself. In a way which seems strange at first sight, Zeitlin finds the Jewish counterpart of Schopenhauer in Rabbi Nahman of Breslau.

Rabbi Nahman describes the evil inclination as a man who comes to a group of adults or children with a closed fist, and offers them what is inside it. They are excited by the prospect of what is contained inside his fist and are prepared to do anything to win it. They do not know that he is duping them, and that, in fact, what is inside this closed fist is nothing.

This story is meant to tell us, as Zeitlin sees it — and shows features in it which are parallel to Schopenhauer's pessimistic position — that pleasure does not really exist, enjoyment does not exist, and the only thing which exists is pain. Joy exists only as a break, or a cancellation, of that suffering or lack. If we now remember what we have learned at the Medieval school of Maimonides, that evil is nothing but a lack or privation, and that real existence is pleasure and joy, we can see the distance between these two positions. Even in the world of Hasidism, or in the literature of the Lithuanian moralists, we hear much about the positive value of pleasure, which is presented to us as something

111

which may be bound up with many different things, not excluding sin, or some low and crude sensations. In itself, though, pleasure belongs to the upper world, and it is a good. Even when it takes crude forms, in itself it is sublime, spiritual and good. Here, however, pleasure, and good itself, has been turned into the lack of true being — into evil.

At the same time, there is something which should surprise us in this comparison between the positions of Schopenhauer and Rabbi Nahman. Schopenhauer regards true reality as cold and full of suffering — and as such, it is the only thing which exists in the world. Rabbi Nahman says that all voices originate in lack, and joy is nothing but filling in the lack. The problem originates, therefore in the dominant existence of evil. As against this state of affairs, Hillel Zeitlin produces what appears to him to be the right and constructive answer, the answer which will tell us what to do with evil, and how far suffering might help us in our constructive and creative activities.

Zeitlin expresses a total opposition to the positivist view, which he detects in the position of Max Nordau, especially in its expression in his book, *Paradoxes*. Nordau, who is well-known for his Zionist activities, for his thought, and for his associations with the world of psychiatry, is used by Zeitlin as a representative of the positivist view, according to which pessimism is nothing but a disease, the result of neurosis, which presages madness. In this context, Nordau adds that Leopardi died of a venereal disease, Heine reached his pessimism after his disease had touched the marrow of his bones, and Byron showed clear symptoms of psychopathology. Thus, pessimism has no rational causes. As distinct from those genuine pessimists, the common people have a healthy instinct, which makes them accept life and its blessings. Zeitlin feels close to Tolstoy, whose views he describes with great sympathy. He accepts the view of Tolstoy that the revolution in man has to come in the wake of suffering and through a recognition of suffering rather than out of an ignorance of suffering or due to a superficial optimism. We must recognize the existence of suffering and overcome it. We must carry on and construct, out of suffering, our new reality.

This analysis reminds us, to a certain degree, of an idea we find in the writings of Soren Kierkegaard. In his writings, we meet with three figures. The first is "aesthetic man" — what we would call today sensuous man, the center of whose life is pleasure. Beside him, there is ethical man, a man who, like Job, having seen or recognized evil, has passed through a revolution in his life and has emerged on the ethical level. Like some of Tolstoy's heroes, he turns the suffering in his life into constructive suffering.

But Kierkegaard also has an additional revolution, symbolized by the story of the sacrifice of Isaac, by the command directed by God to Abraham, a command which turns Abraham from an ethical man to a man of faith. Thus, in a powerful and cruel manner, a second revolution occurs.

The main idea in this analysis is that there are evils which cause a revolution in the life of a man and which change him. This position found its expression in the writings of various thinkers. Zeitlin mentions, in this context, the works of Dostoyevski, in which — especially in *The Brothers Karamazov* — man discovers evil, man discovers prohibitions and questions them, and what transpires later is that the confrontation with evil and with questions which have no answer brings him back to a simple and innocent faith.

We can also find this idea in the works of Jewish thinkers. I shall cite the examples of two interesting personalities, whose books are related, to some degree, to their personal life. The first is Rabbi Moshe Heifetz, author of *Melekhet Mahshevet*, whose commentary on the Torah was greatly influenced by Leibniz. The book is something of a reaction to the death of his son, and it was written after he had passed through the torments associated with it. The second is Samuel David Luzzato, known as *Shadal*, who also lost his only son, Filosseno, but surprisingly, afterwards constructed a world view which is essentially optimistic, albeit with an admixture of sorrow.

In both cases, we are faced with the position of people who have felt deeply the intrusion of evil into their lives, but this feeling did not ruin them. Instead of ruin and destruction, they discovered within themselves the possibility, and sometimes even the strength, to carry on building.

Hillel Zeitlin stresses here the alternatives posed before us by the Torah itself: between life and the good, death and evil. The Torah also says of itself: "Whoso finds me finds life" (Prov. 8:35), thus seeing the positive element in life. But on the other hand we also have the feeling — from the Prophets, through Ecclesiastes, down to the Kabbalah — that Judaism was aware of what Zeitlin describes as *weltschmerz*, the suffering of the world, the problem of evil and the fact that evil exists in our midst.

It is interesting that the answer which maintains that one must carry on and give a practical, rather than a philosophical, answer to the problem of evil, is discovered by Zeitlin precisely in the Book of Ecclesiastes. He was, of course, familiar with those scholarly interpretations which attempted to dissect this book into its various sources and treated it like a field in which various thinkers meet and express their different views — first, the pessimist, and then someone who comes and tries to correct the oppressive general impression.

But Zeitlin believes that the Book of Ecclesiastes must be understood in its full form in which we have it now. One should understand its pessimism as a pessimism which leads to a stage of faith, It is like the pessimism which fell to the part of Job, who saw evil, believed in God, but aired his grievances against Him. Job confronts God, struggles with Him, and does not accept the easy consolation of his companions or their theodicy. Yet he continues to believe in God, struggles with Him and talks to Him, virtually to the end of his days. Here we have a synthesis of all the questions man asks, the questions called by Zeitlin the Jewish question, the Greek question and the Indian question. These are the questions of a man who stares reality in the face and attempts, despite all, to turn suffering itself into one of the constructive constituents of his personality and of his life.

XIII.

The Master of Sorrows

In this last chapter, we reach the end of our survey of the history of one problem in Jewish thought.

In the course of the previous chapters, we have examined a number of positions. We saw some positions which offer a philosophical solution to the problem of evil. We became familiar with the positions of some Medieval philosophers, and saw how some thinkers attempted to turn evil into a source of creation and construction, once they had come to the conclusion that the position of the philosophers is an optimistic illusion which leaves man no possibility of reaction.

We referred sometimes to the positions of the leaders of the Hasidic movement and presented their brand of mysticism. It may be appropriate, at this point, to stress some additional characteristics of this approach, since one can regard the mystical attitude from different points of view. We have seen the mystic who looks at reality and, reacting to it, maintains that there is no evil in the world. Not because there is no evil whatsoever, but because the amount of evil is so small that it should be of no interest to us.

Let us take the example of a boy playing with marbles, who notices that one of his marbles has been lost. For the boy, this is a great loss. Indeed, we find in the writings of the Lithuanian moralists the idea that a man who steals a marble from a boy is like a man who has ruined the house of an adult, since, for the child, the loss of one marble is a tragedy which he cannot assess in an objective manner. The reaction of the mystic is different. He maintains that this is, in fact, no tragedy, since you can and must overcome it. You have to understand the nothingness of loss and of sorrow for loss. Once you have understood this, you will overcome and understand reality in a different manner.

Thus the mystic regards all those people whom we have discussed so far as if they were worried and crying over the loss of dolls and marbles. He regards them as people who have not transcended the minuscule interests of this world and have not learned to think clearly.

The mystic, on the other hand, maintains that there is a possibility of overcoming and transcending the world; of penetrating, as it were, the area of another reality, and the moment I do this, I am above the power of things of this world, including suffering itself. This finds its greatest expression in our love of God and in the feeling that, if God is with you in heaven, what have you on earth? It is the feeling that beyond what seems to be true reality, there is a greater and more beautiful one, and you can move toward it and reach it until you have cancelled your selfhood and your being. Then, when you become part of that different reality, you will see things differently.

This is not exactly a feeling of illusion, nor is it the claim that reality is an illusion and not what it appears to us, but it is a message to man that he can carry on, rise above himself, and then he will see the nothingness of the problems with which he was occupied only yesterday.

For an existentialist like Rabbi Soloveichik, this position would be interpreted as an escapist position — one might say, as philosophical opium or drugs which man takes in order to forget reality.

But this position is not unique to mystics. We find it, for example, in *Olelot Ephraim* by Rabbi Ephraim of Lunschitz, author of *Kli Yakar*, as well as in the works of some of the leaders of Hasidim and other thinkers, who call on man to rise up and follow the true reality.

Against this background, we shall now encounter one of the

great figures of Hasidism, whose conception of reality and whose reaction to the problem of evil was entirely different — Rabbi Nahman of Breslau. The current and popular view of Hasidism regards it as a movement whose attitude to reality is positive, and portrays the Hasid as a man who enjoys drinking spirits, singing and dancing. There is truth in this, but it is not enough to give us the complete picture. Hillel Zeitlin already stressed that the joy of Hasidism did not originate in an ignorance of reality, but often came as a counterweight to the pessimism which comes with a knowledge of reality. This awareness is a hallmark of the doctrine of Rabbi Nahman. There was, perhaps, no man who was more aware of the suffering in this world than Rabbi Nahman.

In one place, Rabbi Nahman writes (or, to be precise, his pupil, Rabbi Nathan, writes in his name): "Now everyone says that there is this world and there is the world to come. We all believe that there is a world to come. Perhaps there is this world in some other world. For what it seems to be is hell, since everyone is always so full of great suffering — and he (R. Nahman) said that this world does not exist at all."

We recall the view of Maimonides and Leibniz concerning possible worlds. There may be some world in which this world exists. It is a possible world. But the world in which we find ourselves, the world which has been realized, is not this world. For our world is a hell, a world in which there is suffering — physical suffering and, as Rabbi Nahman stresses, perhaps more than any other thinker, psychical suffering which is bound up with physical suffering, and, above all, spiritual suffering and madness.

In his reaction to this suffering, Rabbi Nahman says: "And the rule is that one must strive with all one's powers to be always full of joy, since it is in the nature of man to draw himself into melancholy and sorrow because of the blows and ravages of time, and every man is full of torments." And R. Nathan adds: "And he (R. Nahman) spoke to us many times concerning the torments of this world, that all denizens of this world, all of them, are full of sufferings." This is far from the optimism we are accustomed to ascribe to the Hasidic movement when we look at it from the outside. It is the feeling of a

117

man who knows that there are torments, but also knows that one must struggle against suffering and torment. Hence Rabbi Nahman's cry, best known in its Yiddish original "Gewalt, Yiden, zeit nisht meyo'esh!" (Help, Jews! Do not despair!) One of Rabbi Nahman's parables is: "On the matter of joy, in the form of a parable. Sometimes, when people are joyful and dance, they snatch a man who stands outside the circle full of sorrow and melancholy, and draw him against his will into the circle of the dancers. They force him, against his will, to rejoice with them as well." Rabbi Nahman adds: "The same applies to joy; for when a man rejoices, melancholy and suffering depart from his side." Rabbi Nahman puts the man who rejoices and leaves melancholy by his side on a very low level. This is the level of people who dance with joy and leave the sorrowful people by the side. The higher degree is that of the man who strives to chase his melancholy and draw it into the dance, so that it itself will turn into joy.

Our reaction must, therefore, be paradoxical, and the paradox is in the demand that it is not enough for one to rejoice — one must also force melancholy itself to rejoice. This brings us to a reexamination of the whole issue of evil. In the Kabbalah, there is a parable of a snake lying around a treasure. There is a treasure, but in front of it there is a serpent, and thus one cannot reach the treasure itself. It appears that the problem of good and evil, which is not merely the problem of evil but also the problem of suffering as presented by Rabbi Nahman, is what prevents a man from reaching the treasure. Classical theology attempted to find a way of reaching this treasure through faith in God, in observing the order which exists in the universe. This quest is known as the teleological proof. You look at the order of this world and of the heaven and the stars and say to yourself: Who is it that created all those? — or, to be more precise: Who is it that organized and ordered all those? These things do not appear to be the result of some accident, but of an order, of an intention, of some wonderful plan.

But the deeper we go into the problem of evil, the more we find out that this order is far from perfect, and that beside it there is also chaos and there are also problems. Here, man is faced by a difficult problem. This is how we should understand Rabbi Nahman's suggestion that we should draw melancholy itself into our rejoicing. This idea also exists in literature, and it is with this that I would like to end our journey, our quest of pictures in the exhibition of thoughts concerning good and evil.

We find an interesting relation to evil in literature, which is apparently far from philosophy. I would like to refer, in this connection, to two writers who deal with the image of evil and often make a personification of it — that is, of Satan — Agnon and Bashevis-Singer.

In Agnon's work, we often meet with personifications of Satan. I shall mention only one. In his fascinating story, *A Whole Loaf*, we meet with the personality of Grassler, a man whom the narrator claims to have known. Let us quote a few lines. Agnon, the narrator, says: "Mr. Grassler is an acquaintance of mine — one of the most singular of my acquaintances. How long have I known him? I have probably known him ever since I knew myself. It would be no exaggeration to say that from the day I came to know him, our love has never ceased. And, although all the world love him, I can say that I am his favorite more than anyone else. For he has taken much trouble with me and showed me various types of pleasure, and whenever I tire of these pleasures, he amuses me with words of wisdom. "

In another of Agnon's stories, we meet with the figure of Andermann ("another man"), whose name is close enough to a translation of *sitra ahara*, the Other Side. The converse image is that of a doctor, who stands for Moses. But in our story, Grassler appears to fulfill the function of both of these figures, and he is characterized with two kinds of temptation. On the one hand, he tempts with pleasures — the temptation which Rabbi Nahman mentioned (as we saw in a previous chapter) when he told his parable of the man with the closed fist, who comes and promises to give you the things which are inside it, and you undertake all sorts of actions in order to win these things, when you finally discover that there has been nothing there. But Grassler also amuses us with words of wisdom. In these connection, we should remember that

119

Rabbi Nahman was aware that evil is expressed, not only through pleasure, but also through *doubt*. Rabbi Nahman was thus aware of Grassler's other side; that evil is not only physical suffering, but that there is an even greater evil typical of the life of modern man — doubt; doubt as to the meaning of it all, doubt as to man's final aims, and doubt in one's faith. In one place, Rabbi Nahman even depicts for us Satan emerging at night accompanied by all sorts of devils and demons. This is a picture already familiar to us from the Zohar's depiction of evil; but their essence has now changed. These demons, devils and monsters are now the quandaries and doubts which add to the suffering of man. Here we have an embodiment of another aspect of suffering presented to us by Rabbi Nahman.

This aspect finds a fascinating expression, in my view, in the work of Isaac Bashevis-Singer, which I would like to cite as my last example, since it seems to me that in it we find that revolution which consisted in drawing melancholy itself into the circle of the dancers.

There is an interesting story by Bashevis-Singer called *Zaidelus the First*. It is narrated, in the first person, by the evil inclination. We are told in it of a man called Zaidel Cohen, who has no evil inclination. The narrator, the evil inclination, simply does not succeed in clinging to him. He cannot bring him to commit a murder, to steal, or even to stop his study of the Torah. He is a man without hair and without a beard, and therefore, in symbolic language, the Other Side cannot cleave to his body. It transpires that one cannot tempt this Zaidel even to fornicate or to commit any other transgression. What is more, he is rich and devoted to his studies.

The Devil, therefore, cannot trap him, and nothing helps. Satan appears to him through the inner voice of heresy, Satan within man, since Satan already knows what we have learned from Maimonides, since "the same one is Satan, the same one is the evil inclination." He prefers to raise doubts: assume, for example, that there is no God. So what? answers Zaidel. Even his non-existence would be divine, since only God, the cause of all causes, has the ability not to be. This is an interesting remark, which we also find in some books

120

of contemporary radical theology. Zaidel, the Other Side tells us, has only one fault, pride, and Satan exploits it. He promises him that if he converts to Christianity, he will no more be a mere Zaidel, but will rise up and become, no doubt, a pope — Zaidelus the First.

Zaidel turns into a nihilist, to whom everything is equal and there is no judge and no judgment. He only has to follow his own wishes. He becomes a convert to Christianity, and, like many other converts, he searches for libellous materials in the Talmud in order to make a name for himself and rise up in the Christian hierarchy.

At the same time he continues, of course, to study the Talmud —not only in order to advance his cause, but for the sake of study itself. He does not achieve a great position. He ends up by becoming blind, and now Zaidel the son of Sander, or Benedictus Janowski, as he is now called, sits outside churches and begs for charity. He is poor and blind, and all that he remembers is the studies of his youth. He has long forgotten everything which he studied later, and the questions continue to torment him. He has even lost his final ambition, and he now keeps asking himself: "Is there a divine guardian, or is everything matter and disorder? Is there a soul, or is it merely a secretion of the brain?"

Finally, Satan appears before him. Now he appears in his other garb, bringing him his death. Now we witness an interesting conversation. Zaidel asks: "Who are you, the Angel of Death, or Satan?" Satan answers: "Yes, I am the Angel of Death. I have come to take you." Then Zaidel says to him: "If so, if there is hell, this means that there is also God." "No," says the devil. "This is no proof. There can be hell without there being God." But Zaidel says to him: "This is not true. If there is hell, there is God and there is everything. If you exist, He, too, exists. Now I am ready to go to hell." Thus ends the story.

The end of this story comes in order to show us that there is significance within evil, within the abysses of evil — and Bashevis-Singer has dealt with these abysses of evil from all possible angles of observation; from the demonological angle as well as from that of sin. One of the illuminations he brings out is bound up with this very strange and paradoxical leap, which begins by maintaining that

121

evil exists, and even radical evil exists, and this is not merely some evil inclinations or others, but Satan himself, the evil which exists outside us and against the idea of which Buber has protested. He is objective evil. But here we have the paradoxical leap, when we are expected to make our *a fortiori* reasoning: "If you exist, it is clear that He exists." This is Rabbi Nahman's idea in a different version, when we also succeed in drawing the man who is drowned in sorrow and melancholy into the dance which we strive so sadly to dance even after all our suffering — a dance of joy.